Do You Think You'll Like The Wind?

*"If you ever come to Clare and seek her windswept face, take heed
and do not spare to look in every place"*

This book is dedicated to Clare and all its people, old and new.
To Bernie, who always believed, and to Susan and Stephen.

Do You Think You'll Like the Wind?

The Story of a Dublin Family's New Life in County Clare

Paul Murphy

THE COLLINS PRESS

Published by
The Collins Press, Huguenot Quarter, Carey's Lane, Cork.

Printed in Ireland by
Colour Books Ltd., Dublin.

Book Design by Upper Case Ltd., Cork.
Typeset by Upper Case Ltd., Cork

ISBN 1898256039

ABOUT THE AUTHOR

Born in 1957, Paul Murphy grew up in the Dublin suburb of Drimnagh. After leaving school at age fifteen he worked in a variety of jobs. In the 1980s he began writing and had several articles published. In 1990 Paul moved with his family to the isolated village of Kilbaha on the Loop Head peninsula in County Clare on Ireland's west coast. He is now full time administrator with Rural Resettlement Ireland Ltd. Of his adopted home he says: *"It is akin to Provence but without the food, the sun and the glorious houses"*

"This book is for all who have grasped at a dream and for all dreamers who believe they will too some day"

"Paul Murphy is a writer with a story to tell and he tells it with great clarity and precision. If you live in the city and ever wondered about moving to the country, this book will make the journey for you.
If you live in the country and wondered what city folk think of you this book will give you a glimpse of yourself through city eyes."

Alice Taylor.

Do You Think You'll Like the Wind?

The Story of a Dublin Family's New Life in County Clare.

The Collins Press

The Beginning

The distance is nothing; it is only the first step that costs.

Mme. du Deffand.

Chapter 1

The first time I heard a voice that would become very familiar to me in later life was on a cold wet March day in 1990. I sat listening to the Gay Byrne radio show, the driver of a children's double decker play bus, at a travellers halting site in Ballyfermot in Dublin. The programme was being broadcast from Galway. A man was being interviewed about his idea of looking for houses to rent for families who wished to move from the cities of Ireland to empty houses in County Clare on the West coast. His simple dream, he said, was to help find these empty closed up houses and bring life back to depopulated rural areas.

"There are literally thousands of these houses all over the West of Ireland, many in my own village of Kilbaha, just waiting for families to live in them again. For years people have been leaving , or simply dying," he said. "The cities of Ireland, particularly Dublin , have huge waiting lists of families. It is simply allowing people to rear their children in a clean safe environment, thus reducing the burden on city authorities, not to mention the benefit to the families themselves and the rural area to which they move."

What could have been more enticing to me, a person who had always dreamed of moving to the country, than this West Coast sculptor going on to describe the beauty of the Loop Head peninsula in County Clare. Not to mention my being a frustrated would be writer, in a job I felt was going nowhere, with a wife and two small children and a house mortgage of twenty years. The image of a towering lighthouse immediately came into my mind, the only thing I knew about the Loop Head, heard many times on radio as a location during weather reports for storm warnings on the West coast of Ireland. Need he have mentioned anything more than his previous days escapade, that of collecting driftwood along the beach on a Sunday afternoon with his family, while the wild Atlantic ocean rolled onto the shore.

I felt he was talking to myself alone, asking me to consider the dream of moving to one of those houses in the West. I could almost see myself and Bernie, my wife, walking the coastal roads with our two children, Susan and Stephen, stopping to throw stones into the pounding waves and later sitting in a country cottage looking out over the wild landscape.

What city dweller hasn't thought of some day leaving the rough and tumble of urban living, to settle in some idyllic spot away from the troubles of the world. To move to a romantic image of the country must have passed through everyone's mind at some stage during their adult life. But to actually contemplate taking the next step. That of seriously considering contacting someone who has this unusual idea of bringing families from the city to live in rented houses in the West of Ireland. That is what takes it from the realms of fantasy to the hard facts of making a decision and dispelling grand illusions. Not to mention reversing a trend in Irish society going back for hundreds of years, that of people leaving the country areas to flock to the cities.

On that cold March morning looking out the large windows of the old bus I sat on, which Barnardos used for providing pre-school education for travellers, it was not difficult to dream of the romance of a move to the West. The permanent Corporation halting site at Labre Park, where I had spent many such winter mornings, could not have been more removed than the image of another Ireland being described on the radio that morning. The site consisted of a line of about twenty small single-storey houses with a large hard soil clearing in front. This clearing was used variously for old shacks to hold horses or as a sorting ground for the heaps of scrap metal and junk which was brought in and later sold by the young men on the site. Occasionally the clearing was taken up by the cars and caravans of relations visiting for holidays, or well attended funerals on the death of a site dweller.

I had no great love for the actual job of driving the multi-coloured bus. I got on well with those I had to work with, yet I was conscious that while they had chosen to do what they did as a career I had gotten the job primarily because I had a licence to drive a bus. I had been in Barnardos for three years but always felt that I could do more in life than drive a pre-school bus, no matter how necessary that or any other bus driving was. But there were bills to pay and children to feed and although the pay wasn't great, it was a job, which was more than many people had.

However, from the moment I heard Jim Connolly and his dream, unknown to even myself, I was sold. Having written down his address, it was now my task to subtly convince my wife Bernie to feel as I subconsciously did. I could think of nothing else for the whole day and must have cycled the six miles that evening from Donnybrook Garage, where the bus was parked, along the Grand Canal to our home in Drimnagh in record time. When I got home the first thing Bernie asked was whether I had been listening to the Gay Byrne Show that morning and the man talking about moving to the country. We decided to contact him.

Our discussions on moving to the country had been many and varied, yet none of them had concerned a worry about Dublin or the area where we lived. Our reasons if we did move would be for the positive benefits for us rather than the negative aspect of running away from the city. We genuinely loved the house we were living in. It was ours, although we would not own it for another twenty years. Even the trauma of two burglaries had not completely dispelled the safety we felt in it. My mother lived less than one hundred yards from us in the house I had grown up in. She was there if we needed her and on my monthly salary, with a large house mortgage, that was usually about every third week.

Looking back, one of the first things to cross our city-trained suspicious minds was that there must be something in it for this Jim Connolly fella. Maybe his family owned a furniture removal business, or his brother was an estate agent. What reason could he have for wanting to move families from Dublin into his own quiet back yard. Bernie and I decided to write to him and see how it went, mindful of the cuteness of those country people.

But first we had to take out a map of Ireland and look for this Kilbaha he had spoken about. As I pointed along the page to find where the index said it was in county Clare, my finger almost dropped into the Atlantic ocean. We eventually found it on the end of a tongue of land, the Loop Head peninsula, and looking at it the place didn't seem to have land enough for any houses. But if it had a lighthouse it might have room for a few cottages. Having written the letter, we decided we would tell no one of this odd course of action and went on as normal with our lives. We had been living in the Dublin suburb of Drimnagh since shortly after our marriage in 1982 and our two children Susan and Stephen, like ourselves, had never been in the country for more than a week on holiday at one time or another.

3

A week or so after writing we received a type of basic newsletter from Jim Connolly, outlining his scheme to help people move from the city to parts of depopulated Clare. We wrote again, giving my mother's phone number if anything should arise, and went on with our lives as before, with only a slight hope in the back of our minds with regard to moving.In early June, Jim Connolly phoned to say that the perfect house had come up for rent in his own village of Kilbaha. We decided to go to Clare and take a look. We were still uncommitted to any move and viewed the visit at best as information gathering and at worst as a weekend break. My main worry, as we left the children with my mother and took the bus from the warm Saturday afternoon streets of Dublin that June day, was that I would miss too much of the first match in the 1990 World Cup that night. We looked forward to our first trip to county Clare, little aware as we sat on the bus to take us across Ireland, of the change in our lives that was just beginning.

Chapter 2

‘I was born on a Dublin street’ . That line from an old ballad comes to mind when I am asked where I came from in the city. The street was Smithfield, a large cobbled stoned square with a whisky Distillery facing number 47 where we had rooms. (My mother later told me it was a room not rooms.) The paper mills was on one side of our house and Duffy's scrap cars on the other.

I was of a generation in the late nineteen fifties that wasn't really born in a house on any street but in the large maternity wards of public hospitals. In my case it was St. Kevins, now St. James, the sprawling Dublin southside hospital, bounded on one side by James Street and Guinness's Brewery, and on the other by The Grand Canal. Sadly the Grand Canal no longer flows near the hospital, now filled in as a type of walkway, and for some reason St. Kevin fell from grace as far as the hospital was concerned and it became St James's.

Of 47 Smithfield I remember very little, as our family moved to the suburb of Drimnagh when I was four years of age. I have vague memories of some things during my first four years in Smithfield. The horse drawn carts and cattle going up to the Cattle Mart on the North Circular Road and the beggars, as we called them, coming out each day from the nearby Morning Star and Regina Coeli hostels. I remember running away from characters with names like Hairy Lemon, and an old woman we called Mary Bubbles, who passed the steps of our house each day.

The Smithfield and market area remained large in my childhood, as I had many relatives there and returned by 23 bus each day from Drimnagh to school in North King Street and later Brunswick St. or

Brunner. Brunswick Street was of course renowned at the time because Paddy Crosby, of `School around the Corner' fame, was a master in the primary school.

My childhood in Drimnagh was no different from most of the children of my generation in Ireland during the late sixties. There was the ever increasing influence of the Television, not of course as obtrusive as it is today, and certainly not as colourful. The large field which faced our house was where we spent most of every day, and night, playing football. I can never remember a day when we didn't have a ball at our feet.

The field or pitch across the road from our house was owned by Good Counsel G.A.A. Club, and though many of the children in our area played hurling and football for the club, soccer was king among my contemporaries.

Looking back on the late sixties and early seventies of my youth, there were of course many other things than football. I learned to swim in the nearby Canal and also to test a bottle of Smithwicks ale on its banks in my teens. I also learned to first appreciate the innocent joys of ladies along the Bocco or canal bank on late summer evenings.

Although we lived in a city it wasn't until our late teens that we strayed far from the square mile of ground that was lower Drimnagh, Dolphins Barn, and Kilmainham, with its old historical jail on which I would later write a long article, but as a youngester played along its dark corridors, having shaken off the tour guide.

My father worked in the Guinness Brewery all that time and, like many of the other men who worked there as I later found, he had a great appreciation for the produce of his labour. There were many heated rows when I was in my early teens between my father and my elder brother Benny, as my brother was turning to a man, which my father for some reason was unhappy about. As they both got older they mellowed. I ignored all of it anyway, and myself and my younger brothers, Ken, Tony and David, reaped the benefit and freedom that Benny and my sister Marie, like many older children in families at the time, had fought for. It was a normal mad Dublin household.

I had done well in school and enjoyed the place until at thirteen I entered my first year in Secondary at Brunswick Street. In the entrance exam I had secured second place overall among several schools in the area who had to sit this exam because the school had a particularly good reputation and a large catchment area. It was a surprise to me, and to our wonderful teacher at the time Mr. O'Connor, that a boy from the `6B' should get the highest marks in

6

the school.

From then on it was all down-hill as far as school was concerned. On my first morning in Secondary, during a music class, a Christian Brother's answer to boys who could not sing was, firstly to place them at the rear of the class, "with all the other crows," and secondly to strike one of them violently with his fist for not being attentive to the good singers. As well as this, our religious instruction consisted of an aged teacher scratching page after page of the Old Testament onto the blackboard for the whole hour of his class which we would have to copy into a large note-book.

My only memory of this man speaking was his repeating of the old Biblical king `Nebuchadnezzar' as he underlined the strange word for the scribbling silent class of boys which he turned his back to.

In 1972 aged fifteen I left school, against my parent's wishes, and first got a job in a local grocery shop called Bannons. On the first nervous Monday I started work, the smell of stale veg and rubbish at the rear for the bin men made me sick and I hated the place thereafter. But I was fifteen and going to save every penny I earned to become rich.

After a few months I got a job as a storeboy in the Dept. of Posts & Telegraphs Stores department, a good pensionable job someone said. At fifteen it wasn't the most important aspect. I left Mr Bannon with his parting words that the P&T was a dead end and I should stay put. Oddly both Mr Bannon and the old P&T are now gone.

Soon after starting in the P&T I learned that the greatest secret at that time was to do as little as possible, and to always carry a piece of paper wherever you went on the premises, as no one then took any notice of you. I grew from a child to a young man there and at nineteen was taught as part of the work how to drive trucks. I suppose for that it was probably worth the uninteresting years of doing work that didn't seem all too important. In 1979 the P&T went on strike for almost twenty weeks and when it was over I had changed and could not go back to the boredom. I handed in my notice.

During the weeks of the strike I suppose I began to mature. As it continued, week after week, I read every book I could lay my hands on, good and bad. Mostly bad. I would stay up reading when the house was quiet, and not go to bed until the sun was coming up the following morning. In one week alone I had read twenty novels. After those first eventful weeks I promised myself that I would only try to read books that I could learn from, and if I was ever in a position of being out of work, I should try to stick to a normal routine as regards bedtime and rising. I have often done neither, but the books I began to take from the Library made me a little more aware of other things.

After discovering the History and Biography section I knew that for adventure, intrigue, thrills, and even sex, this was the part of the Library to head for.

Having left the P&T in 1980 I drifted into a job as a driver with C.I.E., now called Dublin Bus, calling in on Friday and starting the following Monday. It was during my time there, in 1981, that I met my wife Bernie. We were engaged on the Ist of April 1982, and having discovered to our surprise that it was for real, were married in June 1982. Susan was born in July 1983 and Stephen in November 1985. We took out a mortgage on a house in Drimnagh in 1983 and between leaving C.I.E in 1985 and working for Barnardos as a pre-school bus driver, I worked with my two brothers in shops we leased, selling fruit, veg, fuel and anything else we got cheap enough. After a few years, and before we killed each other, we gave up the shops and became friends again.

Realising in my mid twenties that I was qualified for very little, yet eager to do something, I began to look at myself and see if there was something I could do other than driving a bus for the rest of my life. Many times when I had finished reading a book I had foolishly said that I could do better. I had to start somewhere, so one day in Eason's bookstore I bought a small book titled `Teach Yourself Creative Writing,' by Diana Doubtfire, and set to work. Very soon I realized that this writing game wasn't as easy as I thought. The book did however teach me how to present and supply manuscripts and this was invaluable to me later. I still believe that no one could have, or still can, teach me how to write.

In 1987 I received the first money ever for something I had written, an article on the Dublin Bus Lost Property Office. An article had been one of the exercises in the book on creative writing, and as I worked on the buses I thought that what people left on them by mistake would be a good choice. I had sent it to some newspaper several months previously. When I didn't hear any thing of it I lost interest in writing. Coming across a rough draft of it, some months after the initial enthusiasm, I had it typed and again sent it off, this time to The Irish Press. I was amazed to receive a cheque a few weeks later for it. That was it, I was going to be a writer. Such is the innocence of ignorance.

Chapter 3

Almost seven hours after getting on the bus to take us to West Clare, Bernie and I stiffly alighted, on a warm summer evening in Kilrush, with the knowledge that we would have to go through the misery of that journey again in two days. Jim Connolly met us in Kelly's bar in Kilrush, where he played the piano each Saturday evening. The actual journey had taken all of that seven and a half hours with only short breaks for a cup of tea and changes of buses. Certainly not the best way to charm city people away from all they knew, particularly short bus journeys. It would have taken us less time to fly to America.

At closing time, when Jim had finished playing, we put our bags into his small rusting Citroen and started out on the final leg of the journey to Kilbaha. " Is it much further?" I asked as we trundled from the bright lights of Kilrush into the dark abyss of the surrounding countryside. " Oh no, only about twenty miles," he answered calmly. Twenty miles, I groaned inwardly when I realized he wasn't joking. All Bernie and my untrained eyes remembered of the journey was the searching beams from the car's headlights and the never ending darkness.

When we finally reached Kilbaha, Jim left us with the lady who owned the local B&B and told us to stroll up to his home in the morning, when he would take us to view the house. The lady, Nora Haugh, showed us to our room, at the end of the longest day of travelling in our lives. " Are ye thinking of moving down here?" "Yes, we might be," we answered. "Ye must be mad," she laughed. At 2 A.M. on that Sunday morning, physically shattered, and in the back room of a house enclosed in the dark of the Loop Head peninsula, maybe we were.

They, whoever they are, say that things are never as bad in the morning. So to confuse us all the more, after an enormous breakfast provided by Nora, we saw Kilbaha for the first time. And of course it had to be a beautiful sunny morning. Stepping from the front porch of the B&B, we were literally, and physically, stopped by the sheer splendour of the place.

For the first time, and many times after, I was amazed by its remarkable beauty. In front of us was the wide river Shannon, blue green, with white-tipped waves gently breaking on the rocky shore and reflecting the morning sun. Across the twelve miles of this, Ireland's largest river, and what I had mistakenly presumed was the Atlantic, the Kerry mountains stood high and azure on their side of the estuary. The road into the village of Kilbaha ran atop a lofted rock-river bank, with green fields bounded by high wild-flowered ditches and large stone walls stretching away north and west, all the way to the lighthouse at the land's end. A small fishing pier, with a couple of fading brightly painted boats tethered against its wall, wound into a U-shape on the river, with the ruins of the Big House looking down from a hill above the small bay.

We strolled along the tar road into the village, stopping every now and again to look down the high rocky bank or across the wide river. It was just after 10 o'clock and as the only Mass in the village church was at eleven there were few about, save for an odd passing motorist. These were all curious and slowed to look at the two strangers walking on the road, before waving and speeding along on their journey. We passed the post office and pub, with Haiers sign over the bar, and trying the door to the shop to buy a morning newspaper found it locked. On we walked, around the road by the small bay and tried the door of Keating's shop to find it also locked. The only other buildings in the village were a couple of private houses and we learned later that they were holiday homes only used occasionally. We continued up the hill on the road to the Loop Head lighthouse, in search of the first thatched house on the right, as we had been told, Jim Connolly's. Later on, when returning in the same direction, after mass had finished, it was as if people had come out of hibernation, with children running about, men and women standing about in groups talking and cars parked as if abandoned outside the two shop/pubs.

I suppose, with the value of much later hindsight, we unconsciously made up our minds to move to Kilbaha on the walk to Connolly's that morning. Everything about the place was beautiful and far from what we had imagined the West to be like. To further convince us the house Jim took us to see had one of the nicest views in the area. It was high on a hill, with a rising hedge-enclosed driveway. At the entrance to the curved drive, a sycamore tree stood gently swaying on guard. The house was a squat three-bedroomed bungalow, with three-foot thick walls and two chimneys, of which only one ever had smoke rising through it. This was from a large white Stanley range in the spacious sitting room. In the following winters no amount of fuel shovelled into it could heat the large sitting room. There was no fireplace for the second chimney, but I later found that this was an old 'keep up with the Jones' feature of houses in Clare. Behind the house, sheds rose to the stone walls which ran along three boundaries of the field in which it stood. In front and below the buildings about a half acre of land was covered in overgrown weeds and bush.

We met one of the owners, Michael Tevlin, who along with his twin brother Gerry, was a lighthouse keeper. He showed us through the house, explaining a little about what it possessed, how it would be a year's lease and so on. No decision was expected until, well, two days at least. There was a lot of interest in Jim's scheme.

We also met Kathleen, Jim's wife, and took to her immediately. In fact the whole trip had dispelled any suspicions we may have had about Jim's financial gain from the enterprise. He was a real and active dreamer. They fed us and took us back into Kilkee in the afternoon to catch the bus back to Dublin. Their genuine hope was that we would move. After having only met us that day it was surprising and flattering.

On the bus on the long journey home, the jumble of images of that warm Sunday played across my mind. The things I would see so many times in the future were new and inviting, and in comparison to our life in the city, exciting. The wide river, the rocky shore of the Atlantic, telephone poles blown at slanted angles by the winter winds, a man whitewashing his cottage, the deserted roads, the unusual large crowds after Mass, an old man, Paddy Bán, shaking my hand in reverence to the Dublin football team of the 70s, the new country accents, the narrow tar roads, and the river and sea surrounding all. One abiding memory would be of meeting another old man on his way from the church in Kilbaha that first sunny summer morning. Obviously knowing the reason for the visit of these two strangers he greeted us, and waving his hand to take in the peninsula he asked, as if in ownership, "Well, what do you think of it?", "It's really beautiful." "It is that. But tell me this", he said, leaning towards us conspiratorially, "do ye think ye will like the wind?" We may not have got to like it, but we made its acquaintance many times afterwards.

On Sunday night, the bus driver dropped us grudgingly on the Crumlin Road. It's amazing at the difference of two places on such a small island, yet I always felt it when I later came to Dublin on visits or returned to Kilbaha. It is not as if Kilbaha is in a different country but the same one in another age.

We collected our two children from my mother's and took them sleepily home where they immediately burrowed under the sheets, only staying awake long enough for Stephen to ask if we had bought them anything. We deliberately avoided talking about the trip or our decision on whether to move or not. It was too close to all that had happened anyway and the travelling on the bus would have turned us against ever going near Kilbaha again.

Monday morning is a particularly good day if you are thinking of giving up city life to live in the country. Yet everything had to be gone into. As I have already said we were very happy living in Drimnagh, and all our friends and neighbours where there. Leaving Dublin was not for the negative reason of not liking the place. Although we had many friends in the area the only people we really went out with socially, if we had the money, were either of my four brothers. A country house might be very suitable given that our family had never had such a place in all our lives to visit. I suppose when it came down to it I was more for the move than Bernie, however both of us were aware that if we didn't make the decision to go then we might never do so.

We listed the pros and cons and the pros won with my biased leaning towards them. We were probably not in full control of what was happening, yet in an odd way, somehow doing exactly what we wanted to. And oh the things we would do with our own house in the country. The children would be safe, they'd have a pony to ride if we came into money. We would walk on country roads and stroll on sandy West of Ireland beaches. No more would most of my wages go to pay the mortgage. No more would the children be confined to the back garden for most of the day. Our mad dog could run around to his heart's content and tire himself sufficiently to stay off the furniture. The children would get the almost one to one education that only a private school in Dublin could provide, yet which was normal in small country communities. I would fish, grow all our own vegetables and have a car with the money left over from the sale of the house. And I would finally write that book which would buy us the house we had dreamed of. We had nothing to lose and all to gain, I informed Bernie with conviction.

Looking back over the list she didn't seem to figure all that heavily in it. But we made our list and the ayes had it . I had shut up long enough to allow her to make up her own mind and on Tuesday, two days after visiting Clare for the first time in our lives, we decided to move there. I phoned Jim and his delight was a further boost. I later found he was as happy with every family that moved.

1990 and the first three months

Chapter 4

While Ireland was basking in the glory of the Irish team in Italy that wonderful summer of 1990, we started to make plans to move the two hundred miles to West Clare. People's reaction when we told them varied from envy to disbelief. "I've always wanted to do that", one of Bernie's friends said. "What will you do for money?" asked another. "Where's Kilbaha, in Africa is it?" from yet another. Bernie has only one sister, and her family's reaction appeared to be that I was about to sell her into white slavery. My own family were used to my odd behaviour.

Our house in Drimnagh was advertised and sold before the end of July. It had been only a few weeks since our first visit to Kilbaha and still some weeks away from the children's first time in County Clare. Everything was moving quicker than we could control, even if we wanted to.

The first hitch occurred around that time. The house we were moving to in Clare wouldn't be free until two weeks after we'd left our own. We could always stay with my mother, but what about our furniture? I rang Jim Connolly. " No problem, we'll see if we can put it into the school. Just as long as you're out by September when the kids go back". And that's what we did.

Our furniture sat in the two-roomed schoolhouse in Kilbaha for two weeks until the house was ready. A friend of mine had moved it in a company truck. He couldn't believe the distance Kilbaha was from Dublin and his repeated question after passing through Ennis was, "Jaysus are we not there yet?" I don't know how many times I said nearly, and genuinely believed it.

The weeks between the sale of our house and the move to Clare were passed in a kind of holiday anticipation. We stayed with my mother and father, and their two-bedroomed house was bedlam. My mother had raised six of us there but her carefully planned routine of years after her children's departure was totally disrupted. With some of the money from the sale of our house we could buy a car. I spent most of that time looking for one, and being totally mistrustful of anyone I had dealings with. I was eventually lucky enough to find a Nissan Bluebird with one previous owner, a doctor. There wasn't a drop of blood in the boot and it hasn't given me a minutes trouble since, except to fall apart from sea-induced rust in Kilbaha.

Of the rest of that time I remember little, except for the fact of feeling a sense of freedom seldom experienced before, after I handed in my notice at work. I suppose it was starting to live our dream.

We had planned to move on a weekend but this went against my mother's knowledge of the occult. Because of some old wive's tale she would only let us leave on certain days. 'Saturday flitting is short sitting' and all that. I don't believe in bad luck and all that but I thought we might as well not take any chances at that stage.

On Thursday morning the 23rd of August, (the omens being good) we packed in the stuff that wasn't already sitting in the school in Kilbaha. We loaded myself, Bernie, the kids and the dog, in that order, and left Drimnagh with no hype whatsoever. Next stop the wild West.

That evening after a drive of five hours, with our mad dog romping about the car with excitement, we had the curious sensation of having landed in another age again. It was late summer and the country-side was so peaceful and still that it felt strange. In a city it would have been eerie but in the quiet of Kilbaha, with the tide out, the roads deserted, no sound of cars or people and the evening sun still warm, we started to unwind.

Having called into Jim's, we collected our furniture from the small school in Kilbaha and took it on Martin Haugh's tractor, down past the small overgrown graveyard, through the village and along by the road that leads to Loop Head. About a quarter mile from the village the tractor slowly towed its trailer load of our belongings up the steep driveway to our new home. Although I had driven everything from a bicycle to a bus it was my first time on a tractor. As I had never driven one I was determined to pass the initiation test of travelling along the road on such a vehicle in our new rural area. I held on and tried to look as if I had grown there, probably not too successfully.

It had been a strange type of experience, loading a tractor with all our furniture from the small two-roomed school-house where our children would soon be sitting. Inside, the rooms were full of cuttings, charts and posters, with everything brightly coloured. To see for ourselves that the two teachers obviously took pride in their teaching eased any worries we may have had regarding the children. We had asked before moving what the teaching staff were like and we were pleased with what we had been told.

Anyhow, none of the furniture was broken and the school could go back to looking like a normal place of learning. Jim Connolly and his son Seamus, as well as Martin Haugh and myself, made short work of the removal. We were assisted occasionally by our children and their new friends, Elizabeth, Jim's daughter and her friend Martin Lillis, a neighbour of twelve going on thirty. They would disappear to explore the fields and the cows, wade through the overgrown garden at the front of the house and occasionally return from the undergrowth, looking up at the trailer to ask " Can we help?" " Yes," I would repeat for the umpteenth time, " stay out of the way ". Off they would go again, giggling at the now stale joke, before appearing again from some other direction to ask again.

All our belongings were moved in a few hours and we finished just as the sun was disappearing. As the house was already furnished, we now had two of everything. Two fridges, two cookers, two washing machines and beds all over the place. That night there was a particularly beautiful sunset. After everything was put inside we watched the sun sink behind the hills to the west, seeming to extinguish itself in the Atlantic. (God, the place was getting to me already.)

Later, when the night became cool, we decided it was time for sleep. After the hectic day we'd had, driving down and moving everything, we were only fit for bed and a good night's sleep. But I'm afraid it wasn't to be.

Chapter 5

That first night in Kilbaha, the kids slept better than they had in months. One member of the household however didn't sleep too well at all, our dog Todd. Bernie and I lay listening well into the night to his mournful baying for the comforting sound of cars and cats and noisy neighbours. His loneliness was a little contagious and we felt it for a while during the first dark hours in our new home. On later nights, when the dog was accustomed to the house, the silence would keep us awake for ages. When he did shut up that first night, we eventually nodded off, only to be woken at dawn , before six, by two bouncing kids who wanted to check out the fields, the beach, the rocks, the pier, and on and on.

The next few days were spent trying to sort out boxes and bedclothes, looking for cups and spoons, or dropping the whole lot as the sun beamed and the beach was a few minutes walk away, not ten miles from Dublin on the 32 bus to Portmarnock.

We soon discovered the spot behind the pier at Kilbaha where the sea comes into little sandy inlets bounded by rocks. Other natural secrets of the place were told to us over subsequent days. The square-shaped pool where the sea comes in, and when it recedes the water begins to heat as the sun rises. This little pool was on a sea level ledge under the cliffs at the old house Dun Dalhen. To get to it we had to walk along the cliff top and climb down a precarious winding steep pathway, which frightened the life out of us, but delighted the children. The pool was warm and secluded and was one of the legacies of the big house, along with a small lookout tower which stood a little to the west above it. The pool had followed the building of the tower in the last century we were told. The square-shaped swimming area had been blown out by dynamite so the gentry could have a warmer place than the sea to swim. Having tried the sea and felt its cool waters I knew they were right.

Even behind our very house, the fields rose to a scenic hillock and then fell gently through three more fields to a flat wide rock ledge on the Shannon. It was quiet, deserted, and a peaceful walk in our back garden. Blackberries hung all along the field walls and we spent the second day filling buckets, cans, basins, and our mouths, with the fruit. That evening we made six jars of jam, and afterwards we even ate it. It would be a long time before the holiday atmosphere evaporated.

The second night I decided to check out the Local. 'The New Bar' better known as Jenny's, was the nearest to our house, and I walked to it on a beautiful end of summer evening. As I was heading in that direction, Jenny Keating, the Bar's owner, was driving in ours and I unknowingly passed her on the road as she went to our house with a welcoming box of groceries and goodies for the kids.

When she returned to her post I was already nicely settled, with a pint almost despatched. Jenny served me the next one, and with my change inquired, " Can you sing a bar of a song at all?". When I realised she was serious I said I believed I could and would try later in the evening. I did so then, and many times since. Around the small horseshoe-shaped bar, as people came in from working on their farms or from fishing, we sang song after song to hushed silence, broken only by applause at the end of each rendition, with me trying to think of all the Dublin songs I could, except Molly Malone. In the pubs in Dublin if you sang a song you'd be presumed drunk and expelled from the premises, probably by a barman who had served you all evening, but would ask how you got in that state.

I somehow made my way home safely. I hadn't realized just how dark country roads can be without all those neon lights. It was one of the first surprises. The moon was blanked out by heavy summer clouds but stars glittered in the clear patches. I had never seen so many. For most of the quarter mile I had to walk with my hands in front of me and several times I nearly went over ditches on each side of the road. When dogs came out from farm-houses I prayed they wouldn't make a dart for me, as they would have gotten a chunk before I could even see them.

It was on that first walk home in Kilbaha that I realised why some country people are believers in fairies, ghosts and pishogues. If a branch had brushed my face I would have gone tearing down the road in terror. For the first, and many times after, I was glad to see the light on the top of the hill in our house.

After two weeks in Clare it was time for the children to go to school. Susan had already been in school for two years in Dublin but Stephen would be going for the first time. From our house we could see the school a mile or so across the fields and the sound of the children's voices while at play is carried over the land to where we live.

The number of children attending the year our two started would be the lowest ever, only twenty-three would enrol. Susan would be in a class of four, and Stephen a class of five, and because the two classes were in the same room, Stephen would later start picking up bits and pieces which were years ahead.

God knows where he gets it, but he is the shy one of the family. He'd been talking about going to his new school for weeks, but the minute he saw it the first time that September morning he decided that school life wasn't for him after all. There must be something in the design of schools or some terrible aura of past pupil's terror hovering around, because the moment some kids see school on that first morning they're like quaking cowards going to the gallows.

When I eventually got him moving towards Mrs. Roche, his new teacher, it was in the company of my right leg, which he obviously felt should also accompany him. The other four children in the class were already seated and when he saw he wasn't to be incarcerated in solitary confinement, plus some coaxing from Mrs. Roche, he eventually loosened his grip on my leg. His eyes, however, never left mine. I was well aware that they were saying 'How could you leave me here, you're supposed to be my father?' But leave him I did, and of course Bernie and I worried all day that both of them would settle in and would be O.K.

When I got back to the school that afternoon I saw that I needn't have worried. The younger children got out at two and Susan's class at three. Stephen, however, wouldn't come home, and wanted to stay with Mrs. Roche. I had to drag the little turncoat out of the place. And this on the very first day I met many of the mothers. In fact I was the only man collecting the kids as all the other fathers were working on the farms.

Also during that first few weeks another member of the household began to show signs of insubordination. Our dog 'Todd', a sort of Jack Russell-type mongrel, was bitten by the ranching bug and he took to cattle herding in a big way.

One Saturday evening he got loose and the first inkling we got of his escape was a sound that must have been familiar on the Oregon Trail long ago, but was now coming from the field above our house. We had just come back from a long drive and I was in no humour to go romping through the fields with a crazy dog. When I reached there, with his lead in my hand, he was in the process of stampeding about twenty cows past where I stood. A stout stone wall with barbed wire surrounded this long sloping pasture. I tried calling, whistling and even shouting at the little cur, but he was having too good a time to take any notice of me. I hadn't really taken much note of how big cows actually were when standing so close, as against viewed from a bus window, but I knew the only way to get him out, before the farmer came and shot me, was to get into the field.

With my knees wobbling I had to jump the wall, but on doing so I'd failed to see the cur wheel the cattle at the top of the field and start them down in my direction. Upon landing I almost died with the sight of about ten ton of frenzied beef charging straight for me, with the sole intention of escaping the yapping of that little mongrel, and no regard whatever for anybody in their path.

I made a dive back over the wall just as they thundered past but I caught my trouser leg in the barbed wire. Before I could untangle myself, From my upside down position, Todd had gotten back over and was happily trying to lick my face, with his head slanted as if to ask, 'what the hell are you doing hanging around here?'

When I did eventually get down, I made sure to do as the cows had attempted and give him a good kick up the arse. From then on he had to be tied up and was content to mock them from afar. What he didn't seem to realize was that a four-legged Dublin house alarm was of little use on the Loop Head Peninsula.

Chapter 6

It was in Jenny's, and Haier's Bar across the Bay, that I began to meet some of the local characters of the area. One of the first was a man I called 'The Pirate of Kilbaha,' a blow in like myself, who fished the bay area during the summer months living in a well kept mobile home near the pier. This Irish buccaneer was the nearest thing I was ever likely to see to a real pirate. With his black beard, his rolling gait and tanned complexion, which he told me he acquired from diesel fumes, I had visions of him hoisting 'The Jolly Roger' on his little lobster boat as he sailed out of Kilbaha Harbour to raid the monasteries on the Kerry coast. He had also been one of the first to ask of the state of my mind when I was introduced to him one evening as having moved to the area. " They're all mad around here, so you'll settle in easy enough.

The Pirate has the greatest number of songs of anyone I have ever met, frequently, and without hesitation, belted out in the local bars as host of evening song so to speak. Later in the year, when he takes his winter break from Kilbaha to better paying shores, there's a deadly silence about the place, until his breezy return the following spring.

After our first few weeks in Kilbaha I managed to get him to take me out on the boat with him. I was a virgin sailor, it being not only my first time on a small boat but my first time ever fishing. As we struck out through the choppy waters and cleared the small pier that cool September morning, the Pirate and his son skipped about the deck of the small open-decked boat readying the bait, while I clung to a sturdy fish-smelling post of the exposed cabin. " Is it usually this rough?" I called back to them as the boat rose and fell, in what I imagined to be a heavy sea. The Pirate looked at his son, both barely able to keep from laughing. " Are you feckin joking or what?" he said. I loosened my grip and tried to roll with the boat.

On reaching a line of pots, the Pirate operated a diesel winch, while his son stacked the pots, making sure the line holding them remained untangled. Because of previous rough seas they hadn't been out for a few days and most of the bait had been taken with only two lobster after the days work, another first for me, as I'd never seen one in the flesh before. I was surprised to learn that the lobster could eventually get out of the pots after feeding. Most of the pots had at least one or two orange crabs which the Pirate and his son would toss back over the side, having removed their claws first and thrown them onto the deck. There were also large dogfish in some pots and these were also thrown back in. The Pirate's son obviously had a particular dislike for them, as he would open their jaws, clear his throat and spit in, before twirling them round by the tail and flinging them as far from the boat as possible. I helped as best as I could, taking the dogfish from the pots, but I was a bit squeamish about putting my hand into a space occupied by what are to all intents and purposes small sharks. No wonder he spit into their mouths. I also tried helping to fill the pots with bait but the year-old rotting mackerel they use eventually got to me and I let the Pirate and his saliva-filled first mate complete the job. When we got back they were a bit glum with their two lobster catch but they presented me with a bag of crabs claws with instructions to boil them immediately in salted water for fifteen minutes. When I did cook them that night they boiled over, destroying the cooker and smelling out the house. Crabs claws have been banned.

Thankfully over that initial period our crazy dog seemed to be the only one who had difficulty in re-adjusting. Whether it really felt like a type of extended holiday, or was just the natural way, we somehow settled into a kind of slowing down of life. Time didn't seem to be of importance.

And during that time, as well as encountering the more outgoing characters, we began to get to know some of our new neighbours. I had always had the good fortune to believe that people are basically the same wherever you go, but of course there are a number of local characters who add colour to any area, are shaped by it and therefore would not be found anywhere else.

Such a character is Paddy Blake. Paddy Bán Blake is what you'd call a gentle man as well as a gentleman. Paddy had greeted us on our first visit to Kilbaha, shaking our hands with a warm welcome, praising the Dublin team of the 1970s. A bachelor in his seventies,

Paddy lives in a thatched cottage about three fields to the west of our house. He can be seen any day of the year walking on the roads of the area or in deep contemplation over some field gate or other. His tanned features and pure white hair are a result of his peninsular ramblings but one always knows when he is in residence under his own thatch, by his habit of leaving his old duffle coat, not behind the door, but on the pillar outside the house.

Besides these little quirks, Paddy also has a number of passions in his life. One of them is of course 'the Gaelic' and the other is cards, '45' that is. In conversation with him these two passions can occasionally cross over.

On entering Jenny's Bar of a Sunday evening, if the card players haven't started, he might shout " puck out that ball Jinny". In other words, where's the deck of cards? His conversation is peppered with references to the ball, high fielding and players of old, all of which he wraps up with broad smiles and expansive nods. He's the type of character who literally brightens a room on entry.

'45' I discovered is not only a passion of Paddy's but of most of the older, and many of the younger, men of the area. I can't play the game myself but to sit and watch, particularly when perched behind Paddy, is a nights entertainment in itself. And the six players can give any table an awful hammering.

The first time I witnessed such a game I got one hell of a shock at the first real smack the table received. I was having a drink alone at the bar one night during my first month in Kilbaha. It was the first night the card players had got back together. As it was late September all the tourists, or `Rookers' as they're known, had left the area, and it was now safe for us locals to get back to normal, with the long winter nights stretching ahead.

The card game had been on for a while and was fairly quiet, except for the usual banter of 'Tinkers Deals' or 'Good man Marty' or'Barney'. Then it happened. One of the lads, Thomas I think, hit the table an unmerciful belt along with his expected winning trump. Thinking for a moment I was elsewhere and that all hell was about to break loose, I steadied myself to take cover. Of course the next smack with a better trump and game winning roar reminded me that I was in Jenny's and not some dockside bar. Jenny's daughter who was behind the bar had noticed my reaction to the table thumping and laughingly said, "Sure that's nothing. You'd want to see the hand Thomas was dealt last week. He split the table in two."

Another of the card players, and a non drinker, was Marty Haugh, who farmed at Moneen, as close to the Atlantic as you're likely to get. His son Martin had moved our furniture from the school when we arrived in Clare a short time before. Marty, I was told, was one of the most knowledgeable people with regard to the sea and rod fishing . An evening was arranged for Marty to take Seamus Connolly and myself fishing from the cliffs in the townland of Ross, on the Atlantic coast, during the following week.

The evening Seamus and I called on him we were told he had already left for the coast, a half mile to the East. Light was fading and the wind was beginning to rise as we walked down towards the Atlantic coast in the greying dusk. We crossed the fields to try find him on his usual perch along the cliff. I was carrying a borrowed rod and it was difficult enough to scale the rocks which led to the edge. It was now autumn and that evening the wind had become particularly strong, more so because of the height we were on at the sea coast.

We found him eventually, standing on the final narrow ledge of the last sod of Clare before a huge rocky descent. He waved and called to us, but with the wind we were unable to hear him. To the right and stretching as far as the eye could see, were the beautiful high cliffs of Clare north along the coast towards Galway, while to the left and west was the Loop and its lighthouse, with all around the magnificent Atlantic getting wilder by the minute.

Marty came back to us. "Don't come too near the edge", he warned, and with gestures and hand signals had us follow him to a safer and more sheltered place. This was all for my benefit as he and Seamus had often fished from the spot where Marty had stood. They gave me my instructions as to casting and aim, and moved along the ledge where we stood to fish themselves, and probably get out of the way until I had figured out the rudiments of the reel and this fishing game. Within minutes they were pulling in mackerel and, having removed them from the hooked feathers on their lines, placed them in an empty fertilizer bag.

I had still failed to catch anything but was learning how to cast and getting further and further with each throw. Marty came back to where I stood. "Nothing yet?" He took of his peaked cap and scratched his head, as if to say,'what's wrong with them fish at all.' He pointed to a place just under the cliff. "Try down there Paul, that's where they are."

I tried to land my weight, with the three feathers behind, in the spot among the waves where he had pointed. As I reeled the line through the water and back up I felt the unmistakable jiggle along the rod that told me I had caught something. It was an amazing feeling. The first fish I had ever caught in my life. Here I was, standing on a cliff on the west coast of Clare where so many natives of the place had stood, pulling in three silver Mackerel, the beauty of the coastline to either side, the wild Atlantic facing me, and the wind at my back trying to throw me over the precipice.

We caught forty-eight fish between us that night and Marty gave Seamus and myself all but one, saying he didn't eat more than one now and again. After we had gutted and cleaned the lot we thought there may have been another reason.

Sometimes in the area it is hard to give these fish away because of the ease with which they can be caught. In fact, because my family are not very good fish eaters I tend to fish very little. If they are not to be eaten and enjoyed I would not get any pleasure in catching them. It's only if visitors arrive and wish to go fishing that I would bring them to the cliffs at Ross. And then only to the novice ledge where I had first began with some of the local experts.

Chapter 7

If most of the next chapter sounds like a history, geography and topography lesson, it is probably because it is a little like that, so bear with me, as I for one found it interesting. Having lived in the area for a short while I decided to find out as much about it as possible and what follows is the result of this amateur research and being interested in our new locality.

Kilbaha is not really a village at all, in the Irish sense of village, with a main street of houses and shops to either side. Kilbaha North and South are townlands that cover most of the area at the tip of the Loop Head peninsula and are in the parish of Cross, formerly known as Kilballyowen. The nucleus of the village straddles the main road from Kilkee which winds around Kilbaha Bay and continues out to the Lighthouse. There are two pub/shops, a school, a church and church hall.

Haiers Bar has a shop, petrol pumps and is the local Post Office. It faces south to Kerry across the Bay. It was from Haiers bar that some men left to take part in one of the few incidents which occurred in Clare during the Fenian Rising of 1867.

Jenny's, Keating's or 'The New Bar' is west of Haiers almost on Kilbaha Pier and is also a shop and bar. It boasts the distinction of being the most westerly bar in Clare and a sign on the wall points this out with the line 'Last Pub before New York'. The school, church and Hall are reached by turning right at Haiers and continuing up to the townland of Moneen about half a mile away.

Lobster and some fish are still landed during the summer at the small, most westerly fishing pier in Clare. It is also the first sheltered one on the Shannon.

Kilbaha, or in Irish, Cill Beatach, meaning the 'The Church of the Birch Wood' has had a chequered history and in the last century one religious conflict incident which gained the area attention in Irish and English newspapers just after the Famine period of the late 1840s.

The peninsula pre-Famine had a population of almost 13,000 which decreased by 3000 during the late 1840s, with a possible death toll of over 2000 during the worst years. In each census since then the population of the Loop Head has decreased. One measurement which gives an indication of this are the school numbers in the two-roomed schoolhouse in Kilbaha itself. In 1920 there were over 120 pupils in the school. In 1955 there were 73 children attending. In 1991 23 children enrolled and five of these were from Dublin, two of our own and three of the Fagin family who moved from Dublin to the Shannon estuary at Rinevella about six miles from Kilbaha.

The incident concerning the area which made the papers at the end of the Great Famine was a religious conflict flare up involving some local Protestant ministers, landlords, and the local land agent Marcus Keane on one side, with the new Parish Priest Fr. Michael Meehan and most of his parishioners on the other.

The landlord refused to give a site for a Church to Fr. Meehan, so in 1853 the priest decided to build a type of wooden bathing box on wheels. This was be wheeled to a spot of no man's land between high and low tide on the beach at Kilbaha each Sunday, where Fr Meehan would have shelter while saying Mass. The congregation usually numbered around 300 and knelt along the shore. The landlord had also been evicting tenants for not sending their children to the Protestant schools he had set up. Those who did attend were jeered as 'Soupers' because of the feeding of pupils and their families for attendance, and it is still an insult to call someone by that name in Western areas.

Fr. Meehan himself was said to have cursed these 'Soupers' and his alleged curse in the paper of the time, 'The Clare Journal' was strong enough to strip paint.

For four years, between 1853-1857, the wooden structure, or the 'Ark' as it became known, was used for saying Mass. In all weathers the locals made their way to the Ark each Sunday during that time for mass, marriages baptisms and funerals. When reports of this began to appear in English newspapers, a site for a church was granted and the Ark was placed inside the new church, which stands about a mile from the beach. It is there to this day, in a specially built annex to the south wall of the church.

The former residence of Marcus Keane the agent, Dun Dalhan House, is now a ruin overlooking the pier. The 'big house' was burned down during the early 1920s. To realise what prime sites the gentry had the pick of, all one has to do is stand in the ruins of the old house and look out over the magnificent views from the imposing old debris of another time.

Besides the Ark, the peninsula also boasts a famous lighthouse. The original Loop Head lighthouse was one of six which were built about 1670. There is also one castle or tower house still standing of the original four which stood on the Loop.

Carrigaholt Castle, about 8 miles from Kilbaha, stands overlooking the bay of the same name on the Shannon. The famous Clare Dragoons were first trained in the grounds of Carrigaholt Castle and stories are told locally of the ghosts of the Dragoon Buidh or Yellow Dragoons still seen at night about the castle. They were known as The Yellow Dragoons because of the colour of their tunic facings. The Dragoons left with their leader, Daniel, the 3rd Viscount Clare, after the Battle of the Boyne and fall of Limerick. The ships taking them sailed from Limerick and down the Shannon, passing the castle and their own fields before putting out to the open sea and leaving Clare forever.

The castle today is in fairly good condition and we have many times climbed its stone steps to rise to the always windblown top, and take in the lovely view of the land and river all around. It has a commanding view of the village of Carrigaholt itself and the long sandy beach, probably one the most beautiful beaches and villages in Ireland. Most of the buildings are stone, which face onto two streets meeting at a crossroads. In the village is a fishing co-op where one can get the most wonderful fresh fish at bargain prices. The village also boasts six public houses, and it seems to be the tradition that when there you should visit each, what I call doing `the six churches'. Each pub has a different atmosphere and something special to offer, from good music and craic in Morrissey's, good food in the Long Dock, to tradition in Fennells and Carmody's and whatever your having yourself in Keanes or the Anchor. It is the coming place.

The Atlantic coastline around the Loop Head, particularly the drive from the lighthouse to Kilbaha, or the road from the peninsula into Kilkee by the ruins of one of the sites of another of the four peninsula castles, Dunlicky, is vastly undersold in the tourist sense. It's hard to understand why most people take the road to Moher after crossing on the ferry from Tarbert to Killimer, or landing in Shannon Airport. The drive West from Kilkee has comparable scenery and beauty as well as being a much less commercialised route. But I would say that wouldn't I.

In fact the landscape of the Loop Head had been a surprise from the first time I had seen it. The image I had of the West was probably a postcard image many Dublin people have of the West of Ireland. The picture is of a tired-looking old donkey, with two baskets full of turf on his back, being led by an old man with a peaked cap smoking a pipe. In front of him would be a red-haired child skipping along, and in the background a sloped stony field dotted with yellow furze bushes.

That's the postcard image that I came West with. Of course this area bears no resemblance whatsoever to that image, with the exception of the peaked cap, which all the older men wear. There are very few red-haired children, less donkeys and all the local turf is now gone, with most of the people on the Loop Head owning bog miles away in Doonbeg.

The land on the Loop is fairly level, good land if a little wet at times. Man made drainage ditches slash the landscape for miles all round, more so than in any other place I've seen. Each year in spring the J.C.Bs are at full pelt re-digging and clearing these road and field ditches. Later in the year the machines can be seen sitting like metal birds pecking at the tractor loads of cut grass, then trampling it into the silage of the following winter.

The sea is a constant backdrop which effects everything on the peninsula. At one point the land is so narrow that the area is almost an island and there is something of an insular feeling about the place because of this. The ocean is constantly watched for all aspects of life, from its effect on the land and farming, to the things it may wash up on the strand. Many of the small farmers are also fishermen, though these days there are fewer and fewer lobster and other fish to be caught.

In the winter the storms which are blown in by north and south-westerly winds batter the shore line along the coast in the townlands of Ross and Fodry. Fodry, in Irish, literally means the last sod, it being almost the most westerly townland in County Clare. After these wild Atlantic storms have pounded the coast-line, the remains of the coastal tar roads are strewn with stones and mounds of seaweed. And after each of the violent storms the sea has taken a little more of the man made roads and natural coastline away with its recedes.

When looking across the land itself it brings to mind the level fields of the midlands, although there is nothing of the air of midland prosperity about them. The roads are the small pot-holed ones of the Western Islands, narrow, hemmed in by stone walls and winding to unbelievable endings at some hidden farmsteads. Signposts are vague, turned to wrong directions by constant high winds and swipes from tractor trailers. The houses are invariably single storeyed, with two or three chimneys, of which only one has a fireplace at its base. Over the years the houses have been added to and improved until the original ones are almost unrecognisable. Indeed there are only three thatched cottages left on the peninsula. Thankfully there are none of the hacienda-type bungalows prevalent on the Loop as yet. At the moment there aren't enough people living in the community, so very few need to build new houses.

Chapter 8

If the land of our new home in West Clare was one revelation then the people were another. The first thing to bewilder us were the local surnames. I was surprised, and confused for a time, by the number of locals with the same surnames and first names.

The shorthand used by locals to identify people with the same names can be almost as hard to remember as the names themselves. I found it unusual coming from a city background. It was brought more forcibly home to me when picking my way through the 16th-century ruined church and graveyard of Kilballyowen outside Cross village, six miles from Kilbaha. Many of the headstones in the graveyard are almost two hundred years old, yet they had the same names as young people still living in the area.

Once while talking to one of the locals who stood outside the cemetery, and knowing that his own name was etched on many of the gravestones inside, I mused, "It must be good to be able to know that inside there your ancestors of hundreds of years, and with your very name, are buried". He nodded vacantly and said " It is I suppose, but isn't it better to be outside and know it."

To describe someone can be done by where they live, by their father's name, by what they work at, or even their hobby. To take one name that is usual in the area and explain how the local shorthand can immediately describe just who is being talked about, that of Keating.

Bernard (or Bernie) Keating, Jenny's son, she of 'The New Bar,' is identified should there be a mix up as Bernie of 'The New Bar'. The reason is his cousin is also Bernie Keating. He can be identified, if need be, as Bernie D.J., because of his hobby at a local hotel. This stops him being mixed up with Bernie Keating from Cross, not a cross Bernie Keating, and so on. This is repeated over and over with the other surnames of the area. There are many Keatings and Keanes, Lynch's and Heddermans, Griffins and so on, but there are more Bernards, Patricks and Martins.

Another aspect to get used to almost at once was language. Contrary to what many Dublin people might think, residents in Clare and other counties outside the 'Pale' do indeed speak good English. Many of our first conversations with locals had to be slowed down and repeated several times, on both sides, but we each got the gist of it. Some words in West Clare we will have to use in what we might consider their incorrect pronunciation, otherwise people would not understand who, or what, we are talking about.

Words, as well as local names, are pronounced different to the way we might have said them at first. Thus McInerney is pronounced McNurtney, Crotty is Crutty, Keane is Kane and Walsh is Welsh. The saving grace of all this is there are no McNurtneys, Cruttys, Kanes or Welshes in the area. Once that is realized we all know who we are talking about.

During one of my parent's first visits, a little incident which concerned a lack of understanding in the communication line left my father branded with a name in the area which others would not be too happy to possess. He, however. was delighted to retell it on many occasions afterwards. The gory details are as follows.

My father and mother tore themselves from city life and came to stay with us for a weekend after we had settled. Christy, my father, worked in the Guinness Brewery until his retirement through ill health. What ill health it was supposed to be I'll never know, but Guinness's pay him a pension so maybe they have some idea. Because of his long association with the brewery and their generous parting of the ways, Christy feels he has to support them as often as possible, to keep up the share capital, and protect his pension I suppose. He's as Dublin as the Liffey so it was interesting to see how he took to Kilbaha for the first time. His only other time in the West had been a raid across the Shannon into Galway on receipt of his lump sum on early retirement.

My mother would be happy to rest or walk. She could also take in the lovely scenery, from the back of the car of course, when her bunions began to act up.

The first night I took Christy into Jenny's bar, I knew by his shining eyes, the shift of his dentures and the quick tap of his inside pocket to check for his mouth organ, that he would be applying for life membership.

His first view of Jenny's was probably surprising anyhow for somenone used to the conformity of city pubs. The old bar and shop has much of the merchandise, bottled beverages, and other goods outside the counter and under various benches which surround the oldest pool table ever seen. To get the balls out is almost a game in itself. It has round holes for pockets and if you're lucky enough to pot a ball, not bounce it across the room, its descent into the table sounds like the workings of a chain operated toilet. I hope she always keeps it, as I've seen gangs of tourist children spend hours playing on it, around it and under it. I've done so myself, mostly on it.

But that night Christy settled in, and after a few drinks, played many tunes on his mouth organ to general applause and hushed tones of the small crowd. The patience of the patrons for his playing and my singing is commendable. It was the following night that he sullied his reputation. This came about because of the Dublin/Clare language barrier, his generosity, and his slight hearing difficulty in one ear. Because of these failings, that evening he would leave Jenny's with the unenviable nickname for a pensioner of 'The Dublin Drug Pusher.' The details of his second visit to Jenny's are as follows.

When we entered earlier in the evening there were two regulars at the bar. Both were 'steamed,' as the local term goes, and swaying gently on their respective stools. We sat at the empty fireplace and took no notice of them, other than to see one man continually smoking the other's cigarettes. When the other's fags, and patience, had run out, he told his drinking partner where to go, in very forthright terms. The man without fags then signalled in our direction to be supplied with one.

I don't smoke myself, but Christy has this unusual box-type contraption, which gobbles tobacco and paper, and then spits out a rolled cigarette when the lid is closed down. "You're man there is looking for a cigarette," I told my Dad. "Will you have a roll up?" Christy calls to him, and the man not having understood a word, nods drunkenly. Christy then goes up to him, and when the tobacco and paper are prepared, tries to explain that he should lick his own paper, before the operation can be completed to the highest standards of hygiene in these matters. The man waves his hand, which is taken as a sign to continue regardless, so my father licks the paper, closes the box and out pops a perfect cigarette. For a moment there appeared to be a flicker of movement in the man's hooded eyes. Christy handed him the fag and struck a match to light it. This is where a number of factors already mentioned combined to create the subsequent confusion.

Between the difficulty of lighting a roll up cigarette, the drunken aim of the man's cigarette holding lips, and his growing suspicion of these Dubliners in the first place, the operation was a total failure. He suddenly took the cigarette from his lips and flung it violently across the bar muttering loudly about , "Drugs in the bloody thing!"

Christy resumed his seat beside me and, either not having understood a word spoken, or not having heard a word, his bad ear being in the direction of the mutterings, said, "Doesn't seem to like the roll ups."

Later on when the men had left, I told my dad what had been said. He was most amused, and delighted to have at least one good story to tell of his first visit, when he got back to the Good Counsel club in Drimnagh, and all his other pensioner drug pusher friends.

Chapter 9

The obvious differences in the country are what anyone will tell you having spent more than an hour there. The scenery, the lack of people, the peace and quiet and so on. But silence itself can take as much getting used to as noise, and we found that just as in the song, silence has its own sound.

Of course the source of most of the noise in cities is people, so a lack of them tends to lead to one type of peace and quiet. Where we had lived in Dublin you could walk out your door any evening and be sure to meet someone immediately, whether you knew them or not. There were bound to be people in their gardens or standing in groups talking, or kids playing on the road. Cars would be passing constantly. That was city life except for a few hours of quiet during darkness. It was totally different in West Clare.

When we went for walks in Kilbaha we might go for miles without meeting anyone, except for cattle who would accompany us along the ditch to the end of their field, or huge flocks of birds who swooped in their hundreds around the Loop. Many people from cities wouldn't be able to live a life without constantly being in company or near others. Living where there are few people has to be gotten used to and could only be done over time. The benefits were immeasurable, but not at first apparent.

It was a surprise to us to suddenly realize that we weren't listening to night sounds any more in order to identify them. We had been doing it in our case in the aftermath of our house in Dublin having been broken into twice. We often joked of the number of times I went downstairs in Dublin to investigate some noise or other, banging around for a while to give them a chance to get out. For the first few weeks in Kilbaha we were aware of all the night sounds from the fields. After another few weeks we no longer even noticed them.

And if suspected night noises are attributed to someone trying to take something that doesn't belong to them, in Kilbaha it did not apply. Being protective of what you own is a hard habit to break. Yet the whole idea of people taking something that doesn't belong to them in West Clare is just not considered. Bikes are left at the side of ditches for days, cars with keys in them left untouched, children's toys lying about on walls and in farm gardens, delivery's of coal and building materials on the side of boreens. The fact of even commenting on something such as stealing seems ridiculous. After a few weeks we realised that and, almost unknown to ourselves, we became totally trusting. When we go back to Dublin we have to get back into living as we used to and once more start locking up everything.

Each new morning in Kilbaha the dawn chorus of bird song and cow bellows woke us so we put away our alarm clock for good. After a short time, the morning symphony became a normal background sound as the light of autumn came in the bedroom windows at sunrise. As well as their sounds all types of wild animals appeared at the most unusual of times, animals we had never seen in their natural habitat.

One evening while driving into our gateway a fox appeared in the middle of the driveway. "Daddy look, it's a fox," Susan said, the nature lessons paying off. " Lucky we have no chickens," I said as the fox decided to ignore us and casually disappeared into the foliage along the ditch, his red tail vanishing into the greenery.

We've also seen many unfortunate fox, badgers and hedgehogs along the road who weren't quick enough to miss the speeding cars. For some reason, whether it is the aversion people might have to touch them, or not having the time to stop and move them to the side of the road, they are left where they have been killed. Rabbits can hop out from ditches at any time of the day or night and it is always advisable to slow down after they have exited the road into the grass verge, as they usually hop out again. Not so easily run over are the many magpies and the nippy pine martins, their brown sleek bodies a blur as they rush across the narrow West Clare roads.

One particular evening as darkness fell, our dog began to bark from his post on the hill above the house. It wasn't the usual bark of nonchalance he usually let out and which we had grown used to. This was the type which said, 'come out here now, I'm not messing.' I opened the front door to see him straining at his leash trying to get at a huge badger which was waddling slowly past him, snout to the ground, only stopping once to gaze quizzically at the mad dog, and then waddle on. Down the hill he came, saw me standing at the door, looked me up and down with indifference, and carried on with his side to side amble down our driveway. At the first sight of him I had almost darted into the house. The badger was another animal whose large size surprised me.

Another morning I was surprised to find a large dark net on high poles on bushes in the middle of the overgrown haggard at the front of our house. Later in the day a man with binoculars and high rubber boots strolled into the undergrowth where it stood and began to gently remove the small birds which had become entangled in the fine web. I went down to say hello and see what he was up to. "I'm sorry, I didn't know there was anyone living in the house again", he said when I had introduced myself. He was an ornithologist and every year, he told me, they had been putting up the nets to catch and tag the migrant birds which flew over the Loop or strayed there in anti-climatic storms. Even such rarities as 'Wilsons Petrals' and 'Leaches Petrels' he enthused. Also in stormy weather, birds from Siberia and the U.S.A. were blown into the area. " Do you ever get any back that you have tagged?" I asked. " Not so far, but we've only tagged thirty thousand", he said matter of factly. " They did find some of ours on the continent though", he said with obvious pride. The tagging looked like thankless tedious work and only for true enthusiasts I supposed.

The 'bird-watchers' of the Loop must be the only group of people who are happy to see the huge storms which batter the peninsula during late autumn, winter and spring.

After the storms, groups of bird-watchers checking for rarities, are as common as the stones and seaweed strewn along the beach on the roads of the Loop.

Even during the worst weather, when you would not put your nose to the window, they can be seen, like Marines on manoeuvres, lying along the tops of the cliff at the famous Bridges of Ross. The Bridges, (or Bridge, as one fell into the sea), are a perfect seawatch vantage point. For hours on end the watchers lie with their cameras and binoculars pointed toward the wild Atlantic in unbelievable anticipation. The bird-watchers seem to have the run of the place and are part of the scenery. And there couldn't be a more gentle and environmentally- tuned group of people with regard to an abiding passion.

The place seemed to have that effect on all outsiders who came there. Ourselves and our children became much more aware of nature and its cycle, but the kids learned more about it than I was ever likely to.

They knew the birds and the field animals, and though they would have been taught all this in city schools, living in Kilbaha the children saw many of the birds and wild Irish animals as they would never have seen them in the city. Going home through, and living in, a country area from such nature classes was almost a type of homework. And so soon after our arrival Susan and Stephen became what we would probably never be seen as, locals. Almost at once they rhymed away their city accents in the small, two-roomed schoolhouse. They made friends as only children can, without questions of background or past. Immediately they were visiting farms, attending birthday parties, and taking up music and dancing lessons.

With such a small number in the school they became friends with all the pupils. Of course they made stronger friendships with some more than others, mainly in their own age group. But unlike larger schools, the older children did not ignore or bully the younger ones, even keeping an eye on them at playtime. When you need an extra one to make up the numbers in a game of football any child could fit the bill, and the age limit can be lowered if you are forever short of players.

And unlike larger city schools, the children did not go home to their own friends when school finished. From our house we could see all the pupils homes and farms across the land of the Loop. Their friends in the school were the ones they played with afterwards. The same type of friendship can be seen all through the age groups who have been to the small school in Kilbaha. From teenagers right through to older people, the fact that they have gone to school all those years ago together shows in the type of friendships to be seen in the area. Character failings are often dismissed with a justification of `sure he was always like that, even in school'. Meetings between people who have not met for decades sound like conversations between two people who have crossed paths that very morning. And puzzled queries from an outsider like me about someone can be met with the impatient retort of 'sure didn't I go to school with her'.

The homework our children did was mainly at their own discretion and they often did more than required because as Susan might say, "Denise, or Louise, or Deirdre have probably done the next page," and she would continue to work. Many times because of this friendly rivalry I have had to take books from Susan and tell her to go out and play. I haven't had that problem with Stephen as yet, quite the opposite in fact. And happily because of the lack of numbers, girls are treated and take part in all sports as equals. A wonderful way to create equality is lack of population.

Our attitude to our children also changed. With the freedom we had gained ourselves, we gave them a great deal more of their own. Susan was now cycling to school where a few months before we would not have let go of her hand. They skipped off to play with friends, along roads that have no footpaths, yet other than our natural warnings on road safety, and initially looking after them to see if they behaved, we worried a lot less than when there had been paths to walk on. They learned to trust themselves and never the drivers.

Although they later loved the visits back to Dublin and their extended family, they never considered it as home any more. Kilbaha was where, they innocently said, they would live forever. Once when teasing Susan about moving back to the city she stated, "Ye can if ye like. Me and Stephen will go down to Connolly's and wait for someone to adopt us." Stephen agreed with Susan emphatically, then turning to me he whispered, "Daddy, what's adopt?"

As their accents began to change they could never envisage having lived anywhere else. To myself and Bernie it may have seemed like we were still on holiday, while to them it was just home. They soaked up more about farming than I would ever know. They helped the neighbours with milking, rounded up cows, and acquired a healthy fear of bulls. Where all to us was different, to them it was normal.

In the haggard one day as we tried to clear some of the weeds away Susan called me to look at some crawling creature. On her hunkers in deep concentration she whispered to me, "Come here boy and look at this." "Boy, what do you mean Boy?" "But daddy", she said, standing with impatience, "you know I can't talk Dublin any more", and stomped off up the hill in her muddy wellies. Many parents will remember with sadness a point in their children's lives where they felt innocence had passed. I would remember such times as the awakening of it.

Chapter 10

When October had come and blown itself and our first two months in Kilbaha away I decided to try and do what I had come down for, to write. The Clare area has a particularly strong local paper, *The Clare Champion*, and I thought with the interest being taken in Jim Connolly's resettlement drive, the paper might take a look at some articles I had written with regard to our moving to the West and our initial reaction and how our lives had changed.

The first article was about the move and our first week in Kilbaha. *The Champion* liked it, printed it, and in no time I was the fella from Dublin in the *Champion*. I wrote three articles in all up to Christmas and they printed each in full. These articles gave me an opening for other things and, I suppose, promoted in a way the resettlement scheme being advanced by Jim.

Irish people have a great regard and tolerance for people who think they can write and in West Clare it was no different. I always tried to write things as they happened to us and to quote the names of people and places. It became a type of parochial thing to mention the villages and people on the Loop. And the articles had a positive effect in many ways. On a personal level people took us as having a bit of common sense after having possibly despaired of the madness of city dwellers moving to the country with no jobs, or cattle and land to tend.

One of the local lads who worked for the E.S.B. had to attend courses in Dublin and was shown the articles about his home village. "It's about time something about the place was in the paper", he told me one day, "even if it was written by a 'Jackeen'", he laughed.

I was feeling quite chuffed with myself over the articles, but the old saying about a prophet in his own land was soon brought home. One Friday evening I went to Jenny's for a pint. The second article had been published in that weeks Champion. When I entered a number of the locals, as well as the Pirate, were seated in a huddle reading the paper. I noticed my name on the page and was preening myself for the congratulations which I knew would be showered on me when they saw I had come into the Bar.

Eventually, after some noisy foot shuffling on my part, one of them looked around " Ah Paul, come here now and see if you can read this." With that he handed me the paper and was about to hand me a pair of spectacles.

" Read it, didn't I write it." He took the paper back and looked through the glasses at it again. "Be God, so you did", he said with surprise. " I'd say it's good too. But it's not that. You see what we were trying to figure out was whether Jenny's specs were better than these ones that Jack bought for a tenner in Limerick". Philistines.

As the weather began to turn cold and we eased into our first winter we had our first invasion of mice. Their first appearance was about October, as the winter was creeping in and the West wind began to be a regular caller to the back of the house. One night while we were relaxed in front of a blazing fire in the Stanley Range in our sitting room, from the corner of my eye I saw a little head peep out from under it, have a quick trot around and disappear again. I wasn't sure if I was seeing things.

" Did you see that? "I said to Bernie. " See what?". I was just about to tell her when Susan, having just gone to bed, piped from her boudoir in the room behind the range. " See what Daddy ?" "Just something on the television, go asleep now, "I said. " O.K. goodnight. " I whispered to Bernie of the appearance of our little friend under the range.

Now I have to say at this stage that I would be more squeamish as regards mice than she would. I would not pick a live one up by the tail and put it out the door as she subsequently did many times during that winter. We decided to call our little visitor Henry, in case the children were afraid to sleep should they hear us. "He's only a little field mouse", I assured Bernie in my new found frontier's voice. " I think we should get traps " she said. " For what, Henry is only a field mouse, they're no harm." She agreed to disagree.

A few evenings later Bernie called me out of earshot of the children "You know you said Henry was only a little field mouse?" I nodded. "Well, he may be a field mouse but Henry is either a Henrietta or he has a Henrietta, I saw a few offspring". That was it, traps had to be set. We caught twenty-four up to Christmas, and that was besides the ones which Annie Oakley threw out by the tail. For months everything I picked up was checked to see if it was moving. When the kids discovered the slaughter going on in the house, we had to swear them to secrecy before my mother's visits, as she would not come near the place if she knew. During one of her visits, in the middle of our cull of the mice population in Kilbaha, myself, Bernie and the kids would sit in smiling innocence while my mother cocked her ear after another trap sprung. "Noise, what noise?"

The kids started a graveyard after we had caught a number of mice. The actual burial ground is probably one of the most beautiful of its type, high on a rise in a field level with our house, and overlooking the whole peninsula and the roads which bisect it.

Under the brambles in this little corner the children chose, there are now several little crosses and stones from the beach, all surrounded by wild flowers, some wilting, others newly picked. The burial ground now holds the mice, a dead bird, Tweed, a sickly pup born to Lassie, the neighbours sheepdog, one of a litter of four delivered by Lassie in our hay barn. And later in the same spot we had to bury Lassie herself. Lassie was not only a regular visitor to our front door, as well as a delivering mother in our hay barn, but this friendly old collie was probably the first friend the kids had, and one of first to shake hands (or paws in her case) with the children. This happened during our first days when the kids on running outside one evening came upon Lassie sitting quietly outside the door. " Mammy there's a dog outside", Susan called in." Don't go near him, he might bite." " Ah Mammy look" Susan said, as Lassie, almost in answer to the warning, lifted her paw to shake our delighted children's hands.

From then on she was a regular visitor for snacks at the front door, as we found out she had been for years before our arrival. She studiously ignored our mad mongrel who strained at his length of rope just out of reach of getting at her. After her final litter of pups Lassie was a little slower and didn't muscle in on the food given to the pups by us. When they were a few months old, she left them with us in the barn, only returning to sleep there after dark and rise to leave in the morning at the sound of our tap running to fill the kettle.

One morning she didn't show and the children came in to tell us she was under the hay and she wasn't moving. When we put the children into the house I went to the hay barn to check. She had burrowed into the loose hay and passed away quietly near her growing pups. We told Mary Griffin, her owner, the sad news. That evening Michael, her son, and I took Lassie from the barn and buried her beside where we had put her sickly pup Tweed some weeks before.

The rain was teeming down as we chopped out the heavy wet soil in silence. We placed the 13-year-old Lassie in and covered her with the heavy clay. The faces of Susan and Stephen were pressed against the glass of our front door looking out on their small graveyard. When I had washed the muck from my boots and come in to do the same with my hands, Stephen stood beside me at the sink. " Now Lassie will be ᵇle to feed Tweed. But Daddy, em, will Holy God hold Tweed up to er so she'll be able to eat?". " I suppose so," I answered. He was ferring to the time before the weakening Tweed had died, when ᵁsan had to hold her up to the standing Lassie to suckle.

•

Chapter 11

Just before our first Christmas in Kilbaha, the media began to take a keen interest in the resettlement scheme. The number of families moving was increasing each month after Jim Connolly's talk on Radio with Gay Byrne. The newspapers now wanted to talk to these latter day frontier families. Because we were only a few hundred yards from Jim we became one of the token Dublin families to interview, and although I revelled in the attention, Bernie would literally shake at the prospect of an interview of any kind. We really didn't know what all the fuss was about anyway.

The first newspaper to print anything on the scheme was the Clare Champion, which did an excellent article on Dan & Breda O'Brien and their eight lovely children. They were the first family to move and they set up home in the village of Coolmeen, about thirty miles east of Kilbaha, in a house at the crossroads.

Our family were the second and as the national media took an interest, we all became quite good at interviews. Over that time *The Irish Times, Daily Star, Evening Herald, Irish Independent, Irish Press, Sunday World* and later *London Times, Independent, Philadelphia Inquirer* and German papers all came to interview the families. Naturally many of their questions were along the same lines. Why did you move? Was Dublin a terrible place? Would you ever go back? How did the locals take to you and so on. We answered as honestly as possible each time and it was great practise for when the Radio and T.V. crews arrived later.

All the media people who did come down over that initial period, and later on, were genuinely ordinary with no prima donnas, as you'd expect from among the more famous presenters. We had some good nights with many of them and several solemnly pledged to return on their own steam. Of course they're were many characters, particularly the photographers.

On one occasion an award-winning photographer for an English paper decided that he would like to take a colour shot of our family as the sun went down behind us at the Loop Head lighthouse. Sundown was approximately 8 p.m., and it being only five thirty he invited us to go for a drink to pass an hour before tea. Bernie declined but I decided to be sociable. At eight o'clock, as the evening quickly settled, myself and the photographer, both the worse for wear, tried to figure out in which direction the sun would disappear, while Bernie looked on quietly fuming. Those photo's were never used. I heard they were a little out of focus.

On another occasion an Irish photographer brought along his guitar after his day's work. He was a gifted singer and musician and let me play my own G,C, and D, as well at a session in Haiers Bar in Kilbaha. I meant to tell him before he left that Maureen Haier had mentioned a weekly spot, unaware of his being a photographer.

After the series of articles for the Clare Champion, Sean Keating, a local councillor and former chairman of Clare County Council, asked me if I would consider writing a history of the peninsula which had never been done. Of course it wasn't only the articles which prompted him, but also a discussion we had about a history article I had written about Kilmainham Gaol. I told Sean I would be very interested in doing something on the history of the Loop Head area and Sean said he would investigate getting some funds for research.

But meanwhile it was now December and we had something far more important to get over, Christmas. Not only that, but would he, could he, that man in red, get out to the wilds of West Clare, to get toys to our two distracted children. " But Daddy does he know we moved"? asked Susan."But Daddy does he know where Kilbaha is?" from Stephen."But Daddy can he get down through a Range instead of a chimney"? from Susan. " But Daddy what if he leaves our toys in Drimnagh", from Stephen. "And Daddy will he give us everything we asked for in our letter," from Stephen, who incidentally wants to be an accountant when he grows up.

Christmas Eve took a little more planning in Kilbaha than it had in Drimnagh the previous year. Oh we had a huge tree in the corner and all our cards and decorations accumulated over the years were hanging in organised chaos about the house. But this year there would be no mother dear around the corner with big wall presses and no searching little hands. This year Kathleen Connolly, Jim's wife, and her secret presses were a drive away in the darkness.

"Where are you going Daddy?" as I left, from the two sleigh-expecting guards at the window after dark on Christmas Eve. "Daddy's just going for a message", from Bernie. "Are you going to Jenny's?" from Susan. Out of the mouth of babes. When they dropped off I went to collect the booty. Later, when everything was quiet, the plastic bags had ceased to crinkle, batteries had been installed and heaps of gifts separated to each side by guard dog and chain link fence, I did take a detour to Jenny's for a deserved beverage. O.K. I know Bernie deserved one too.

Jenny's, or Haier's Bar, like many others in West Clare on Christmas Eve, is the third stop after Shannon or Dublin. The first is to kiss Mam and Dad and the second is Christmas Eve Mass. In Jenny's I hardly knew anyone but most seemed to know me. I was soon in the bosom of friends who know what it is like to be having a beer for the first time on Christmas Eve away from what was home. I will always try to spend a few minutes in that place on that night each year.

On the way home I stopped outside our house which looks out over the land and houses for miles. All was darkness as usual except for the orange glow from the street lamp which Jenny's and Haier's merit because of their being a business premises. Moneen Church street light I could also see across the fields. Tonight, however, each of the many cottages as far as the eye could see had a tiny yellow candle glow burning in every window. Every house had lit these candles with their message of welcome to the newborn baby and for the sons and daughters home for Christmas. I suppose they also glowed for the ones who couldn't make it home this year. That first Christmas morning in Kilbaha, the children discovered the scope of distance and generosity of Santa. He had made it with all they asked for. When we managed to pull them away from the toys and feed and wash them, they reluctantly went with Bernie to the church, while I set about putting my hands into unmentionable turkey cavities.

We had dinner as normal, but before doing so we rang our families on our newly installed and very expensive phone. When living in Dublin my family always gathered in my mother's house to exchange gifts on Christmas morning. This year we spoke to them all and didn't feel too bad as we would be returning for a visit in a few days.

Our first St. Stephen's Day was almost as looked forward to as Christmas Day itself had been. We had been told that the 26th of December in Clare is much like the 31st of October is in Dublin, Halloween without the bonfires. The same type of dressing up and calling to houses is the norm on the `The Wren' as on `Halloween'. `The Wren' or the `The Ran' as it's pronounced here, is supposed to be a day of music and dancing by the Wren Boys in each house which they call to. I was told that years ago the West Clare Wren was taken much more serious than today.

Dennis Liddane, a local folklorist, and old Wren Boy himself, told me of his days when a young boy in the area and the elaborate planning that went into the most important day of the holiday period. Months before the first items needed would be picked out while the autumn threshing was in full swing. The best sheafs would be chosen to make the costumes worn by the Wren Boys on the day. Next the lads would hunt down a wild goat, catch him, despatch him and, not use his guts for garters, but his hide for Bodhrans. These would be played with gusto on the day in question.

On Stephen's day itself a Wren, having been captured that morning or previous evening, would also be despatched and hung on a furze bush. Dennis wouldn't let me in on how they actually caught the Wren but with the end result I wasn't too curious. In the old days the Wren Boys would pick a Wattle Man or latter day cashier, who would be responsible for the collection of any coppers that might be donated on their journey. This was a most sought after position according to Dennis as it was taken for granted that the Wattle Man would check the takings, and also his own share from a secret pocket. After the day of visiting and collecting, a household in the area would be promised a few coppers for the use of the kitchen for a Hop. This was usually an old batchelor who in the end received nothing but the joy of the company. There would then be what's called 'A night till morning'.

The description of the Wren we were filled with previous to our first St Stephen's day in Kilbaha bore little resemblance to the actual day when it arrived. We had been told to expect much the same with the exception of the transport used. In the past it had been the horse and cart, then the tractor, and now the car or van. We were prepared. We had food and drink, the fire lit and the kitchen table well back.

On Stephen's morning, looking out the kitchen window, west to the slight rise on the Loop and north to the Atlantic, we could see that it would be unlikely that anyone would be venturing forth this day. We had a real storm, one of the type we had been warned of by an old man on a fine June morning which now seemed so long ago.

The Atlantic was almost white for miles from the shore and the sea at Fodry and Ross across the fields from us was in a rage. The land west to the Lighthouse was blanked out by sheets of driving rain which blasted about the house for the day. E.S.B. lines were down, as they often were in storms, but quickly restored. During the day some brave youngsters, dressed in old clothes with strands of windswept hay stuffed into their collars and hats, struggled up our driveway. On opening our door they immediately burst into song, usually ballads sung at the top of their voices, while they looked at their shoes, all to the accompaniment of the wind. None would come in, and after thanking us profusely for the pound coins, they flew down the hill pushed by the breeze. Those new pound coins cost me a fortune. The Wren itself would not be out we were told. Next year, we told the kids, weather permitting.

A few days before Christmas I'd had to call on Dennis Liddane, the already spoken of wren boy, in connection with some comedy scripts he asked me to write for a show the local youth club, Kilballyowen, of which he was leader, rehearsed every year. They put on one of the shows each year in competition with other Clare youth clubs. I was calling to go over some of the ideas for the script. He lives about six miles from us, just outside the village of Cross, and is a dairy farmer. When I knocked on his door it was already dark. His young daughter told me he was above in the cabin. By this time I knew where the cabin, or shed, was and made my way across the muddy farmyard towards the faint light spilling from the slightly open door at the other side of the yard. I reached the door and opened it wider.

Sitting on a stool in the middle of the floor was Dennis's wife Mary. At her feet was a large bucket of water, surrounded by a pile of ever growing goose feathers. On her lap a recently deceased large goose, who had met his end I now saw by means of a large kitchen knife which Dennis was beckoning me to enter with. Mary had the goose between her knees and it was being plucked with obvious skill. In one corner several more very dead geese were waiting to be plucked and in the other some who had yet to meet their end huddled in obvious fear.

"Come in Paul and welcome" Dennis said. I entered, skirting the immediate area of the knife. Mary was dunking the goose into the water again, softening the feathers which made it easier for plucking. Dennis, no doubt aware of my reaction to the slaughter, matter of factly said to me, "I wonder if you'd just hold this big one here, while I cut his throat and finish him off as they say." I told him that although I would eat most types of meat I was a vegetarian where the killing of them was concerned. He was faintly amused, as I suppose most country people are, at city people's attitude to where meat comes from, and how it makes its way to our table.

After some more teasing from Dennis I managed to steer him outside in the pool of light from the shed and conclude our business. When I left he was wiping the knife in a tuft of grass before re-entering. The last sound I heard before climbing into the car was the geese, who started up again as the shed door closed in the light.

A few days after our first Christmas in Kilbaha we made our first trip back to Dublin. When we had been thinking of moving to Kilbaha, we had promised ourselves that we would return to Dublin every six weeks or so to acclimatise to country living slowly. That plan had soon been forgotten and we had to make the time to go back after five months. Naturally in such a short time nothing had changed, except us of course. For the first time in our lives we didn't feel at home in the city. We got the usual slagging of 'culchies' and were asked were we up for the January sales. The friends we met on the visit noticed little change in us other than that I spoke of people in Clare as if they were known to them and that I had gotten very cheeky. Me, cheeky. They're always picking on us country people.

1991 and the first full year

Winged time glides on insensibly and decieves us ; and there is nothing more fleeting than years'

. . .Ovid

Chapter 12

In the first weeks of January, when we returned from Dublin, I started to play football again with some of the local lads a couple of evenings a week. Ten or twelve playing soccer outside the Church Hall in Kilbaha, with two arc lamps usually used for the farmyard, strung up on posts and illuminating the tarmac road and square of rough concrete outside the hall. I started playing with years of soccer behind me and an idea that these lads had only played Gaelic and had little skill on the ground. That was soon dispelled and when I played I was most times puffing behind, but getting fit.

As I said I also got involved with the local youth club, Kilballyowen, who met in the hall outside where we played ball. Kilballyowen have about thirty members and Dennis Liddane ran the club for the teenage boys and girls who meet each Friday. Each year Dennis and Margaret Considine, another glutton for punishment, put together a show in which the youth clubs of the county participate. It is a type of teenage 'Tops of the Town' and the winners go from local to provincial to national finals. When they heard I had dabbled in writing comedy sketches, I was willingly roped in.

Kilballyowen, I soon discovered, are the type of sprint finishers rather than long distance runners, when it comes to rehearsal and showtime. For the two weeks after Christmas it was organised madness trying to get the show together with everyone rehearsing day and night, weekends included. I had written a good deal of the show, Margaret and Dennis had whipped them into shape and the kids were talented and ready to go for the first heats which were to be held in Kilmihil in Clare on the 21st of January. As the night of the variety show

51

approached I was looking forward to seeing my own words come to life and hopefully being laughed at. Faith however was to step in and make sure I would not see that show, or the next, in fact any of their performances for many weeks.

The pain was the worse thing I can ever remember. Worse than any kick ever, and I had received many in my years of playing football. Worse than all of the kicks put together, and yet it had happened so simply. It was Monday night the 14th January. Seamus Connolly called as usual at about 8 p.m for us to go playing soccer. As we left the house we could see a mile or so across to the hall in the clear dark night, the spotlights already in place, their pools of light distinctive across the fields. Each evening after football I had limped home sore from the two hours outdoor soccer played at a furious pace.

" Don't come limping in again tonight" were Bernie's prophetic parting words that evening.

There were about ten playing and for over an hour it was up and down and I was sweating, as I wished, in my jersey and tracksuit bottoms. At about 9.30 PM, as we were deciding whether to pack it in for the night, our side being well behind, someone passed the ball along the wing. This side of the pitch sloped onto a tar road north toward the other goal. I ran after the ball, which gathered speed on the slope and I was chased by one of the other side, Jack Gibson. As I reached the endline and caught up with the ball, my idea was to put my left foot on it, pull it back past the oncoming Jack and kick it across the goal with my right foot.

Whatever happened, whether it was the slope, a stone on the road, the ball, or the movement of my body in a different direction, it didn't work. When I placed my left leg down to stop it, the ball shot in towards my right foot, I fell straight down and with my lower leg pointing away from me, and my foot the otherway, the ankle snapped. The noise was audible, but my screams much more so. For about ten minutes, knowing how badly I had broken it, I would allow no one to move me.

Through the haze of pain it slowly dawned on me that there would not be the sound of an ambulance and the comforting presence of ambulance staff and a stretcher within ten minutes. I was fifty miles from the nearest hospital, lying with a broken ankle on a West Clare road. I knew I'd have to get to a hospital but the thought of the journey was almost as worrying. All the time the lads remained silent and did as I wished, but after ten minutes decided I'd had enough time.

Bernie Keating pulled his car alongside and I was gently hoisted into the front seat. We drove to his house and he phoned the local doctor to see about a sedative for the journey but was told to get to the hospital as soon as possible. Jenny came out from the shop and put some cushions under my mucky left runner, remarking on my white complexion. Looking down on my left leg I saw it was swollen hugely as far as the knee. We were on our way within minutes, Bernie Keating driving and Seamus, who had been to my house with the news, sitting in the back.

It was an hour's drive to Ennis hospital, but thankfully the numbness had taken away much of the pain. On reaching the hospital I was put into a wheelchair and brought straight to x-ray. The nurse removed my runners, covered with dung from retrieving the ball from a field earlier on, and I was placed on the table. It's odd how in times of extreme sickness or pain you feel very little embarrassment. The X-rays, according to the radiologist, showed I had two breaks but the casualty doctor later said only one. I was sent home with some crutches, pain-killer and told to return on Thursday when the swelling had reduced and a cast could be put on.

I lay at home on the sofa for two days feeling sorry for myself, remembering all the days in boring jobs when I had wished for even a broken finger. Margaret Considine and some of the youth club cast paid a visit and I was able to ensure them that I would try to make it on the Friday, the day after I had my full cast put on. That wasn't to be either.

The following Thursday, Seamus Connolly drove me to Ennis Hospital and I limped in to see the orthopaedic consultant before having my full cast put on. When I sat down at his desk he removed my X-rays from the envelope and looked at them through the light from the window. I then saw a doctor lose his temper for the first time in my life. Quietly, as you'd expect.

He took no notice of me as he lifted the phone and proceeded to berate whoever had been on duty the first time I came. "This man should not have been let leave the hospital. He should have gone straight to Croom. This is disgraceful". As he rattled on and on I looked down at my poor foot and wondered whether I was going to hold onto it at all. After his phone lecture, his looking at the X-rays again, this time on the machine, he noticed myself, along with my poor leg, were still in the room. " Mr. Murphy, you have two breaks, what's called a Potts Fracture, it's usual in these cases to operate and place screws in the ankle to help it knit". Hello again leg, I thought with relief. " You'll be kept here tonight and go to Croom tomorrow, if they have a bed" "Where is Croom?" I asked. " Outside Limerick, on the Cork road.

They're very good". They were.

I told Seamus and he headed off, coming back that evening, bringing Bernie to visit and some clothes for my hospital stay. Two hundred miles driving in one day. I'm sure he was sorry I ever moved to the West. He, of course, would never think that way.

The next morning I left Ennis. I was put into an ambulance for the first time in my life. Come to think of it, I'd been doing a lot of things for the first time since moving to Kilbaha, including smashing up my ankle. We changed ambulances again at Limerick Regional and ended up in Croom that evening. On reaching Croom Orthopaedic I was put into a bed with my leg up on a block to look down and mock me. After ten minutes I was visited by Mr. McMahon, one of the surgeons. "Is the theatre open?", he asked the matron beside him, with my leg in his hand, taking no notice of the person at the other end of it. She shook her head. " Back to Limerick Regional," said the doctor, "get them to reset the ankle". Back we went.

Back in the Limerick Regional all was pandemonium. It was Friday night. An Indian doctor appeared with a large syringe to put me under, but when asleep, in my minds eye I can still see him mangling my ankle in his hands like a wrestler, putting the bones back into place. " O.K. now?" he asked when I woke. " Yes " I lied, gritting my teeth, and we were on our way back to Croom in another ambulance. Four in one day.

The following Wednesday I lay outside the operating theatre. The surgeon was to decide if the swelling had gone down enough to operate and put screws into the ankle to help it knit. Mr. McMahon come out in his green overalls. He picked up the leg "Right," he mumbled through his green mask. The anaesthetist nodded, and I nodded off. When I awoke another doctor stood over my head. I remembered thinking, why don't they ever stand where you can see them? " No pain now?" My gurgled scream told him otherwise. Out I went again, riding on a cloud of morphine.

Thankfully, because of the distance Croom was from everyone I knew, there was no one looking down on me smiling and saying, 'everything all right now', as I painfully came too in the recovery ward. Later on I would be very glad of any visitors, as I tried to look invisible when every bed in the ward was surrounded by gangs of grape-clustering, sweet-bearing relatives. The abiding memories afterwards were the severe pain, the lack of sleep for almost a week, and the inability to pee. That took two days and was only eventually brought on when the nurses turned on all the taps in the ward and I stood with the help of an attendant, and no inhibitions, while I filled the metal bottle to the brim. I cried with the pain of getting into and out of a seat for other toilet duties but was selfishly comforted by knowing I was not near as injured as some of the other poor patients.

From being sick and in pain and not wanting to move during that week, when the Gulf War started and I imagined Scuds coming through the window in my helpless state, I slowly became a little better and in less pain and wanting to get home. For the first time really, I realized home was now Kilbaha.

Jim Connolly collected me and the nursing staff transferred their skill and compassion to the man getting into my bed. It was now the beginning of February and we had been living in Kilbaha for five months.

Chapter 13

For the first week after coming home from hospital I sat like an invalid, with a blanket round me, trying to keep warm at the range. February 1991 was the most awfully cold month of the year with constant lashing wind and rain. There were storms that had made the one on Stephen's Day seem like an April shower. The land was blanked out by day after day of driving rain, and in the nearby town of Kilkee the sea destroyed the front, ripping up concrete slabs all along the strand and even turning over cars on the promenade. The weather about matched my mood. Added to the cold was the fact that I had lost weight and not having my usual supply of winter blubber I felt the cold more so. I had many visits and condolences. Paddy Bán Blake came quietly and apologetically, slipping a book from his pocket under my blanket as I lay on the sofa. 'Biddy Earley,''The Wise Woman of Feakle.' A book on the ways of a countrywoman who knew of things not of this world. Marty Lillis, another near neighbour, came to call quite often. Marty had little time for books and reading or such, being a man of the soil and of nature. On his first visit after my home-coming he stood at the door and took in the figure in the blanket. Gauging my self pity he comforted me with wide eyes and head shakes, accompanied by intakes of breath to the side of the mouth. " You look shook boy", he said with a demeanor which seemed to hold out little hope of my survival. Johnny Dunne came to visit me the second day after I had come home from hospital. The saving grace of being incapacitated in our house in Kilbaha was the beautiful view from any window, even in atrocious weather. I was hopping around for just such a look one afternoon and had made it

into the kitchen. While resting, I leaned on the kitchen press, puffing away and misting the window as I recovered. Coming up our steep driveway, almost as slow as I had made it to the window, was Johnny Dunne. Johnny is an elderly bachelor who lives alone in a house to the east of ours. From our first meeting during the autumn he had spoken to us as if we had never lived anywhere else. The reason for his slow ascent up our driveway was the many operations he had endured on his knees in the very hospital I had just left. They made it very difficult for him to bend his legs and to walk up hills or sit into cars. He did make it to the top of the drive and when I let him in we both sat with a sigh on the sofa, not talking for a few moments. " How are you? " he puffed eventually. " Stiff," I said, " and you?"
" SStiff " he said using two s's. Brothers in arms, or legs."I brought you a bottle of beer ", he said, taking two from an old shopping bag. "Will you have one"? I asked " Oh no, not at all ", he answered, no doubt feeling to take one would be a removal of half his gift. I didn't have one either. " Leave the empties in Jenny's " he said. He then put two bars of chocolate on the table. " For the little one's." We chatted of most important subjects, such as the weather and locals and the weather. When darkness was falling I suggested he should make his way home before the pitch black of February settled on the Kilbaha Road. " Oh I'm alright ", he said, pulling a bicycle torch from the pocket of his overcoat. When Johnny did leave, I watched his torch slowly see-saw down the drive and onto the main road, turning right and east towards his own house. It took a little time for him to make it and I stood at the door until he reached his. In Kilbaha nothing would be likely to happen anyway as he had walked the roads all his life and knew to get up on the ditch if a car came. But if he could take the trouble to come up our drive I could stand at the door until he made it home. On Marty Lillis's visits, we planned about his digging the large garden, or 'haggard' as he called it, at the front of our house. Marty works for Clare County Council mending the roads of the Loop Head. He may have little time for books or learning, but has an uncanny eye for the weather and all things natural. The Tevlin's, who own our house, had a J.C.B. come in late February and tear out the accumulated brambles and weeds of twenty years. Limping out on my crutches I could now look down on the $1/4$ acre of clear black earth which Marty was soon putting into ridges and spreading wheelbarrows of manure on. It was a wonderful sight to see cultivated earth below our house where before there had only been weeds and brambles. On Good Friday we put in the potatoes and onions. We, I use indiscriminately, as I supervised, knowing nothing

about it. Marty put down six ridges of spuds and covered them with the straw-laced manure, followed by soil. They were each about sixty feet long so we thought we would have enough come September to last to Christmas at least. The smell of the newly dug soil, the wet heavy feel of it and the perfect symmetry of the ridges to the surrounding area were all a type of natural magic to me. That Good Friday was a beautiful crisp sunny day and as Marty stuck in the seed potatoes, three in a row, Packy Keating, Jenny's husband, came by and stopped to look over the ditch. " How are ye?" By his demeanor he was obviously gearing up for a spot of fun. " Marty, you should know that nothing will ever grow that's planted on a Good Friday" . Marty studiously and busily ignored him. After a few more quips to which there was no reply Packy went off laughing. Thankfully he was wrong about nothing growing. During that spring I pestered everyone to learn about crops and how they should be looked after, particularly Kathleen Connolly, who has always grown her own. It was a beautiful thing to see lines of straight, green, tough potato stalks appear. Weeding between them however, while on crutches, is murder, and when I mistook them for weeds, I was thankful the potato stalks were difficult to pull up. Later I put down peas, turnips, carrots, french beans, spring onions, lettuce and sprouts to various degrees of success. I only needed the first year to figure out what was worth growing and what was difficult. Marty, while bringing new life to the garden, campaigned endlessly about bringing new life to our family. During the spring he seemed to be constantly worried about our, or should I say Bernie's, future childbearing capacity. He is a constant advocate of procreation. "Are ye sleeping in bed or what?" he would demand, almost outraged at the thought. "I have a sore leg Marty," I would tease. "Sore leg, sore leg. What sore leg?" he'd thunder, "the school is going to close unless ye start lying up close. Have she not got a loose coat or what?" As can be seen by the sentiments, it was a chauvinist argument which Bernie took little notice of. Only when I continually teased the unsuspecting Marty would she tell us to shut up and put us both out.

Chapter 14

During the cold February of 1991, a meeting was held in Kilrush to decide whether FAS would sponsor a community response project to research and write a history of the Loop Head. The idea for the history, which Sean Keating had asked me about before Christmas, now seemed in the dim past after all that had happened. I was surprised to find that the course was agreed on by Bill McInerney and Tom Mitchell of FAS at the meeting and I was to be employed as co-ordinator from the end of February. We had to provide a premises and this was eventually to be a portacabin provided by Golden Vale at their creamery at Bella about seven miles from Kilbaha. Almost without trying I was now employed again.

I was the only employee as yet and the premises where we were to be based was not in a good state. Being on crutches I could do little about it. Even the task of researching the history of the area was a daunting prospect. To be honest, I didn't have a clue, although the eventual publication can speak for itself.

I was really in the dark until I had completed a co-ordinator's course in Limerick, and that ten weeks after the course had begun. But that was a long way from the start of the research.

The announcement of the course starting was printed in the *Clare Champion* the week previous to its start, and also, as is essential, it was announced at Mass in the four churches of Carrigaholt and Cross, the parishes of which Kilbaha is a part. Our group were to be called Carrigaholt and Cross Heritage Group after the parishes on which the book was to be written, we hoped. For most of the research the heritage group consisted of myself, Sean Keating and the trainees and it ceased to exist after the research.

On the first cold Monday morning in late February I limped into the dilapidated portacabin, having been driven there by my man Seamus Connolly. And for months until I could drive I was driven without a murmur. After three weeks of looking for people to start on the course I was still the only one, but there was a rumour that one lad might be interested and would call that morning to inquire.

I stood in the quiet wooden room, which is literally miles from anywhere. The nearest shop is over a mile away and the nearest library, which is where we would start and have to spend a lot of time, was eight miles away in Kilkee. All around the building are fields and ditches, bleak and grey on that winter morning. Once inside, looking around I again saw the sad state of the premises. Most of the windows were rotting and broken with no glass. The front door consisted of a few crooked planks that were swaying in the cold easterly breeze. There was no heating, no water, and therefore no working toilet. A grimy pool of water completely covered the centre of the room, having blown in through the broken windows, and sat like a moat between myself and the lone desk and pile of rusted steel chairs on the other side.

I eventually limped around, took one of the chairs down from the pile, sat down and put my copy book full of course ideas on the desk. Looking around again I despaired of ever writing a word on the history of the parishes or of being in a lower mood as regard the place. I was soon proved wrong.

There was a hesitant knock on the door and as I shifted around shouting to who it was to come in, the rusted chair on which I sat completely collapsed. The thin aluminium legs did the splits and I ended up on my arse in the middle of the pool of water, with my crutches to either side of me like oars, and the water seeping into my trousers and plaster cast. The lad who entered, John Garvey, could do nothing but laugh uncontrollably from what passed for the front door. And that I knew was the lowest point. How in God's name were we to write a history of the place. But we were here and we now had one trainee. Only five to go. I felt like Yul Brynner in The Magnificent Seven. I slowly and carefully got up off the ground. It was the first and last time I fell while on crutches.

It was around this time that the first T.V. crew landed in Kilbaha with regard to the Resettlement Scheme. They were an R.T.E. regional report crew, with Alistair Jackson the interviewer. After interviewing myself and Bernie on the reasons for our moving to the West and how we had adjusted, they decided to get some outside shots. " You have to be doing something normal ", Alistair explained, " maybe you could carry some logs into the house ", he said. " Well, we don't really have many logs around here, there's no trees," Bernie said, " but if you want us to look normal we could be coming back up the hill after collecting the post." Our letters are delivered by Kitty Clancy, the post lady from Kilrush, who beeps from her Hiace at the bottom of the hill if we have any letters. " The post will be fine", they said. God we were getting very professional weren't we.

We took some letters from the glass case, and with me struggling up and down that hill on crutches, puffing heavily for take after take, we looked normal. We made the six o'clock regional report a few Sundays later. We had our fifteen minutes of fame we thought, but there was to be much more.

The course researching the history of the Loop trundled along under my questionable guidance. Bernie had to start when, after several weeks, we were in danger of closing due to lack of numbers. Although unemployment is as bad in the west as in the cities the actual number on the live register, which we had to employ on the course, was very small in the Kilbaha area. When there's no work for young people on the Loop Head they usually head off to family or friends in England or the U.S.A. seeking employment. Thus there were few to take up places on the course. We got most of the trainees from Kilkee and after initial teething problems, including a trainee throwing another through one of the recently replaced windows, we were starting to get a little more done. The history was going to cover many things about the two parishes on the Loop, which stretch from the lighthouse at the western end, to Kilkee in the east, and cover an area of about forty square miles.

Some of the subjects I wanted to write about included the famine, religion, schools, music, sport and a ringfort survey of the peninsula, which was a waste of time until we were allowed employ an archaeologist, Robert Chapple, at a later stage.

One particular thing I was very interested in was the interviewing and taping of many of the older people in the area for the chapter on folklore. We eventually interviewed over twenty of these men and women, ranging in age from 70 to 93. Only in one case did someone refuse, asking me " What in Gods name would a man from Dublin know about the history of this place?" She had me there.

With a list of questions made up by the trainees, I set off one morning with two of them, a teenage boy and girl, to interview our first person. I was to leave them to do the interview but I ended up doing it and others until they got over their shyness.

We knocked at Thomas Keane's door. Thomas was 87 years old and lived at Kiltrellig near Kilbaha. He was a tall strong-looking man, with a soft hat, and a pipe in permanent residence on his chin. The door of the house, which faces the main road, remained open except in the worst of weather.

We sat in his old kitchen, with the door open and a March wind humming about the room. As we froze, the interviewers and myself, Thomas puffed away at his pipe contentedly, only stopping to lean forward and ask me to repeat a question because of his bad hearing. "As long as the working man had his baccy, Mr. Murphy, he was happy", was his firm belief. For some reason he addressed me as Mr. Murphy while I, a lad a third his age, called him Thomas. Paul wasn't a name that came easily to the older people in the area.

With Paddy Bán Blake, a sprightly O.A.P., it was the same formula. Paddy had been a friend since we had moved to the area and was only too delighted to impart the knowledge he had stored for just such an occasion. We called on him and he greeted us with glee. " You're welcome Mr. Murphy, you're welcome. And the boy and the girl, welcome", he said in reference to the two mute teenagers with me. He stood warming his bottom at a turf fire in a huge traditional west Clare fireplace, while we plugged in a tape. His door also remained open as always and the view across the wet April land of Kilbaha from the hill where his house stands, although very beautiful, only served to make us feel more cold. He was obviously well used to the open doorway and once planted at the big hearth he needed no prompting from us as regards interviewing. " Do you see that table Mr. Murphy?" he pointed. " My Daddy told me that at that very table a boy had spuds the size of gooseberries and they were hitting him in the eye with water, and him going out racking stones".

As he went on I realised he was talking of an incident during the Famine of the late 1840's, of someone sitting at his table before going out to work on the roads. Racking, or breaking stones, was one of the tasks the starving people were employed at to enable them to buy food. It was to him, and he made it for us, a modern tale. He named the boy, where his house was and how he died. " Wasn't it no wonder they died", he finished, "with spuds the size of gooseberries and them digging roads." We were entranced. Well, I was anyway.

Many times with the older people we talked to, the last century was brought in to meet us in their small kitchens, the time of the troubles of 1916 to 1922 was spoken of as if it were yesterday, and a type of regretable innocence of these old people's youth was repeatedly lamented for its passing. A Franciscan Friar, Fr. Senan Hedderman, aged 93, originally from the village of Cross on the Loop Head, now living in Ennis, wrote his early life for us in the most beautiful handwriting I have ever seen. It was the same in his presence in the Friary later as with all the others. History brought out to meet us, much of it told with a lively comical slant. Fr. Senan related many stories, but his final words in relation to music and dancing in his house at the turn of the century remained with me after. " My father played the tin whistle. After theology and philosophy and all that, I could not even play a penny tin whistle. I think I could have been a better man if I did." He laughed with the pure hilarity of truth.

Nora Haugh, whom Bernie and another trainee interviewed, had been the first person we met in Kilbaha. Nora owned the B&B we stayed in the first night we had come to see our house. Nora is an amazing lady. Small, always in widow's black, she does more work than a group of gangers would in a week. She digs her own haggard, grows all her own vegetables, cuts her winter's supply of turf, makes homemade wine from anything available, runs the B&B, and operates a hackney.

When we taped her most of the sounds when replayed consisted of Bernie's laughter. She spoke of weddings and pishogues and good and bad luck of long ago . On the weddings Bernie had one question to finish off the interview. Where did the young couple long ago head off to on honeymoon, if anywhere? " Did the newly weds go anywhere after the wedding?" Bernie asked. " What do you mean", Nora said patiently."Did they go anywhere after the wedding day, that night?" "Course they did girl", Nora said, " they went to bed."

Chapter 15

In April, still limping about, but with great agility, the call came from on high to Jim Connolly. Gaybo and The Late Late Show on television beckoned for Jim and his families. Jim, Ann O'Keefe, David O'Brien, Mick Daly, Eddie Needham and myself were to go up on a show the following week.

On the Friday morning Jim and I left Kilbaha in a hired minibus, with him driving, and began to pick up the others from all over Clare. It was like going up on holidays and when we got to the luxurious rooms paid for by R.T.E. in Jury's Hotel in Ballsbridge it certainly felt like it. That evening we all met in the lobby, scrubbed clean and shining, and sat down to have our meal in Jury's before heading out to Donnybrook about 8.30.pm. The Late Late here we come. We were taken downstairs to the Green or Hospitality Room to await our entrance. The Late Late Show show started and we watched it on the large screen in the room. I have to say that this 'Green Room', as I don't know if there's another one, was a major disappointment to me. I had expected plush chairs, subdued lighting, cocktails on demand and so on. What I saw was the large screen, rows of chairs, and a table with two ladies detailed to administer spirits, warm beer and stout, but only after the show, naturally.

About ten o'clock, as our nerves began to tingle and stomachs turn, we were given the nod and told to expect to go on after the next commercial break. We were brought through a number of corridors and in behind the guests seating area. Maura Connolly, Gay's personal assistant, was there to calm us down and tell us to be natural. Oddly, Maura is a regular visitor to Kilbaha, having relatives there, and we have often met her on holiday. She gave us our seating arrangements, Eddie Needham at the end, Ann O'Keefe next, me, as I was still on crutches, and then Jim. The break came and we entered the lions den and we were on. I managed to sit and put the crutches away behind the seats and then start to take notice of the place before we came back on air.

Naturally the first thing is to look at Gay for the very first time in the flesh. Of course he was smaller than he appeared on T.V., and he looked unusual to me with all his make up on. Then I had a look around at the audience. They were much closer than they appear on television and there was no need for microphones for them to hear anything said in the studio. The two tiers of seating are also very small in comparison to how you see them on T.V. And all around, even while the show is on air, the camera-men, floor staff, and the director, are constantly moving, signalling, quietly making faces and forever busy. Gay, as anyone will see who's been there, is a consummate performer. When asking questions he has the knack of keeping his attention on the guest while also communicating at times, on and off screen, with the crew and audience around him and also watching the monitors. All this is taken in in the first few moments.

Then we were back on air and Gay talked to us for the first time after the quick hello as we sat. The questions were along the same lines as we had answered in the other media interviews we had done and the fifteen minutes passed quicker than I have ever experienced. The audience joined in and asked some questions and some phone callers also rang in. It was quite ironic that one of the callers said he could not understand why Dublin families would want to move to the country as he found Dublin people very nice having himself moved there from Belfast. I managed to answer that we also found Dublin people nice but were not leaving the people, but the city. And Eddie Needham, two seats from me asked, quite legitimately, why he who had left Belfast, could question someone about leaving another city.

When our time was up we all felt deflated as we left the panel, thinking we didn't say as much as we had wished and wishing it had went on for a few minutes more. The show continued as we went up to have our make up removed.

" You were all great", the make up girls told us and that lifted us a little. After that it was down to the 'Green Room' to receive our refreshments, but only sparingly. Gay came in after the show and was relaxed and friendly just like any of the guests. He was still there when we had left to go back to Jury's where we were sure to get a drink, even if we had to pay two pound a pint for it.

In Jury's we felt we had walked into a party and having all got a seat together, someone signed for a drink on their room number. After that we were like millionaires who had come through the Sahara. We signed for it all on our RTE rooms. It must have been about 4 am. when we got to bed. But we'd have to pay for it in the morning.

Early the following day Jim pulled the minibus to the hotel door. We gave our keys up and piled in, most of us the worse for wear. David O'Brien asked Jim to hold on while he thanked the hotel on our behalf for their hospitality. After a few minutes he was still at the desk. Soon after he came out. " All the drinks we signed for have to be paid" he said shrugging. That news made us a little more sick than we already felt.

We had little enough cash but Jim Connolly had his cheque book. He went in to pay. We would all contribute to the bill when we got back to Clare. It seems that RTE pay for room and meals only, which was generous enough, but something we didn't know, being naive country people.

" How much was it", we asked as Jim sat back in.

" Well one round alone was fifty pounds". And Jim didn't even drink. As the bus made its way up the Grand Canal and out towards the Naas Road all was silent. Jim Connolly suddenly burst out laughing. "Dave", he said, "if we go to a hotel again, remind me to tell you not to thank too many people, will you?". Poor Dave had to listen to it for the whole drive back.

It rained all the way to Clare but it felt like a type of welcoming and cleansing of the city from me. It was dark and still wet when I got home and Bernie took my bag as I put my crutches to the ground and limped in from the minibus. Now it was back to normal. It was good to return from the unnaturally false world of T.V. and hotels which we had left behind.

66

Chapter 16

As spring and early summer of 1991 came, the garden, or haggard, was beautiful as the fresh new greens of things growing appeared all over the tilled soil. As time wore on vegetables began to replace the wet black earth in the dark square we looked down on from our house. The whole works of the garden and nature, of which it was a part, was completely new to me. The nearest I had come to it had been the clearing of a small patch in our front garden in Drimnagh when it became overgrown with weeds. Our city back garden was overgrown for years because no one except the near neighbours could look into it. On moving to Clare it seemed somehow sacriligious not to grow some of the food we would eat, and it had always been one of the tenets of our move.

As I was still incapacitated to a great degree Marty Lillis came often to our haggard, after his day's work on the roads for the County Council. Many times I watched him trench the potatoes, throwing up the spadefuls of earth around the new stalks with deft flicks of the shovel. Later trying to do it myself I learned just how good he was. Often he went straight to the garden and did what had to be done without coming near the house. The only sign of his presence was his bike thrown against the ditch at the bottom of our boreen. There was never a question of his accepting any money for all the hours he would put in then and in the future. His reply was always, " sure your good yourself." His way of saying that his labour was given on a barter basis.

On the lst of May I put my crutches into the boot of my own car and began to limp around. After a few weeks I started to get stronger and limp less and less. To this day the screws are still in the ankle and will only be removed if they are causing pain. I could also drive again and the Connolly's could stop worrying about having to ferry me around.

During the month of May the garden exploded into life, but so also did the weeds. I cursed so many times my vow not to use weed-killer and cursed again while using a brush to spread Bluestone, a presumably almost natural substance, over the potato stalks to prevent blight. I didn't use weed-killer, but I did have to spread slug pellets when all the green was being chewed up.

When one day I put my hand into the warm moist soil and found to my joy a few small potatoes I immediately took them up to the house and washed them for boiling, looking at them for ages. Skin and all later, they were delicious. The first thing I had ever grown to eat, even if it was through the surrogate Marty.

Once able to stand on my own, I could work on the potato crop myself. Doing so, I began to discover the inherent skills possessed by Marty and other men of the soil. But it was was hard tiring work in the learning.

It was a coincidence that during the trenching and later harvesting of the potato crop, we were also researching the history of the famine on the peninsula. Many times I stopped and stood with my calloused hands leaning on the shovel, and thought of the people who had done exactly the same in this same place one hundred and fifty years before. I could imagine them, as I had done, digging up the ground I now dug and discovering to their horror only blackened tubers. The utter hopelessness of someone doing so can hardly be imagined by someone like myself, who if the spuds do fail, can walk down the road and buy a four stone bag in the shop. To stand on the very land where, in the past, if there were no potatoes there was death, was a strange feeling. It seemed easier to write the chapter in our book of that period by having experienced the physical act of growing our own.

Onions and peas were a success, as were swedes and french beans and sprouts. Carrot seeds were put down never to be seen again. Everything really did taste totally fresh and different, but having somewhere to store harvested food would later prove a problem. But never again could we enjoy the bland-tasting, unnaturally clean vegetables not from our garden.

Many times during the late spring as my own crop began to grow I would walk along the road, a few fields to the west, where Paddy Bán was cultivating his own ridges above his thatched cottage. He made the lines straight and true while I leaned against the wall listening to his tips on 'the praiti' or potato. During our conferences many other subjects would receive our attention. One evening the subject drifted around to the 'troubles' and the 'War of Independence' when he was a young boy.

"Down there, on that very road, I saw a truck load of Free State soldiers rushing back to the Loop," he said pointing down the hill, and, as in all his relating of stories I looked below, half expecting to see the truck grinding past. The talk came around to the troubles in the North and our agreement that it wasn't the same thing as had occured in the South earlier in the century. At this time there was no talk of a ceasefire. " I wonder will we ever own our own country again," he mused. " Not by the gun anyway," I said, "it will only be if the majority want it." "You're right, but they never will I suppose." I decided to pull his leg a little with a notion in regard to the North. "You know Paddy, that every year in the North there are more Catholics born per head of population than Protestants." He looked at me strangely, not sure where this kind of talk was leading, but I continued. "Well in fifty years, if the Catholics stick to their religion, and their hobby, they'll keep multiplying and there will be more of them, so they will be able to vote themselves into the Republic, God help them. Now what I would recommend is that the I.R.A put down their guns, go home to their wives, and start right away." I said wives in deference to Paddy's orthodox views on such things. The comprehension of such an enjoyable solution to the Irish problem slowly dawned on him. His face blossomed into a smile. "I get you now, oh I get you now. Oh yes. And Paul," he said, stamping the spade into the soil, "you're right." The next week the Middle East was on the agenda.

For Bernie, myself, and the trainees, the early beautiful summer was a real test for all of us. Looking out from the building where the research was carried on, with the computers and piles of papers and maps, across stone walls and green fields covered with wild-flowers bathed in warm sunshine for days on end, was a real contrast from the modern facilities within. During that time we had to leave the kids with the Connolly's as myself and Bernie were working. Each day they went with Kathleen Connolly and a group of other children to swim behind Kilbaha Pier. Once , sometimes twice a day, this motley crew of Kathleen, four children and the dogs trooped east from Connolly's down the warm summer roads of the Loop to the pier.

Along the shore behind Kilbaha pier the sea comes into little sandy inlets where the children could swim in safety. Susan was a natural, but Stephen would not put his toe near the water and gave everyone heart failure playing around on the rocks with Connolly's dogs. There was Buide, a calculating old lady, and Woody, who got his name from a jazz musician, but could have just as easily got it for his love of chasing sticks. Stephen had great fun throwing bits of wood all over the rocks and into the sea where the ever-chasing Woody would follow. The following summer and every one after would be unfairly measured against the first.

Chapter 17

On the history course during the summer we were told by FAS that we could employ an archaeologist to research the ringforts and churches on the Peninsula. I found it an unusual experience checking C.V.s and interviewing third-level graduates, having not even sat the Inter myself. Still I don't think they noticed.

Robert Chapple, a young archaeological graduate, was eventually employed as an assistant and immediately tore into a survey of the ringforts, exhausting all the trainees, now mostly girls.

On one occasion they politely and femininely decided to down tools because of his zeal. "Please don't send us out again Paul, we'll put everything on the computer", they pleaded. "We're not dressed for all that walking across fields". "Yeah we were drenched yesterday". "We're sore". "But it's a lovely day", I said, " surely you don't want to sit in here do you?" There was no reply. "I'll go myself", I said, feigning annoyance, but glad to get out for a while. "You'd send a poor cripple out to climb ditches, my God", I groaned as a parting gesture and emphasised the limp. All to no avail, they ignored me.

Once outside I asked Robert how far we had to go. "Only a couple of miles. Killinny." " We'll take the car", I said. Robert's job was to check and measure all the archaeological sites, including ringforts, and write the first chapter of the book. As each was checked and measured they would be marked in a map and entered into the computer.

We parked at the gate to the fields we would cross to check on the forts marked on the 1922 Ordnance Survey Maps. " Will we check with the farmer?" Robert asked.

"How many sites have we" I said. "Just one". We decided to tramp across and get it measured quickly as the farmhouse was a good deal away and we would only take a few minutes. The field in front of us had been cut for hay and in the far corner a large stack of small square bales were covered with loose hay and tied with rope. The next field, where the ringfort stood, was the same except for a green uncut patch around the fort.

As we reached halfway across the first field, a tractor came bumping down the small road followed by an open-backed truck. They stopped at the entrance to the field. As my car was blocking the gate, we went back. We did so with a little trepidation as we knew that although the farmers were always willing to allow us cross their lands, we should really have asked.

"How are ye lads?" the man on the tractor said as we reached the gate. We explained who we were. "Oh the Heritage people", he smiled impishly. He was young and athletic looking, with skin tanned from hours in the sun.

"Are you the Murphy man", he said after turning into the field. "I am." We shook hands. " And you're measuring the forts?" "If they're still there", I said. "And why wouldn't they? Tell me", he continued, again with the smile, "do you usually ask for permission before you cross the land? " I looked at Robert. " Yes, always." he lied. " Well we only had one fort to check and we didn't think," I was saying as the farmer cut me off.

" Oh sure that's alright, no bother, but the only thing is that, seeing that you're here, and seeing that you didn't ask, I'm afraid I'm going to have to ask you to do something." "What?" "Help us load the lorry with hay," he laughed. "Oh yeah, no problem", myself and Robert looked at each other, relieved. Such fools.

Three hundred bales had to be loaded from both fields. The truck was parked beside the stacks and we started to throw up the square heavy bales with hay forks. As the stack in the fields diminished in height, those in the truck increased. We threw the first lot almost in unison with the farmer and truck driver but near the end our strength was gone and myself and Robert were unable to lift any more. Our eyes were red and sore with the hay and dust, we couldn't lift our arms and we constantly slipped between bales as the ones we lifted toppled back over our shoulders on the forks. The farmer, Vincent Hedderman, had a fine time watching us.

After a few hours the truck was loaded and tied down. "Would ye like a cup of tea?", Vincent asked. We nodded, unable to do anything else. "Follow me up to the house so." "Can we come on the tractor?" I asked tiredly.

Before we entered the kitchen Robert stopped me. "In future if I have to walk miles for permission to go onto someone's land I will". I agreed. After tea and fresh ham sandwiches we decided to go and measure the ringfort. "Have you any more forts on your land other than the one in the second field?", I asked Vincent. "No", he answered. "Thanks be to God!" We trudged out to the sound of laughter from the kitchen. Months after we were still sore.

If I had thought that a few hours loading hay onto a truck was to be the summit of physical torture in West Clare, I had yet to spend a day on the bog with the sadistic Marty. Jim Connolly gave us a bank of turf to cut and save for the following winter, and I, not knowing a thing about the bog, was advised to get expert help for the cutting. I went back to Marty one evening to broach the subject. " Marty, I have a bog which I need someone to cut." "I'll do that Paul, no bother. You're good yourself, and we have to help the neighbours." It was then that Marty had to consult his mental filofax. Monday to Friday were out, he would be working on the roads. He was off Thursday but it was a holy day and he couldn't work. Saturday so. No, Saturday he was painting for a man in Doonbeg. He couldn't do it Sunday, Mass day. How about the following Saturday? It was agreed, once I cleared the bank of turf before hand.

During the week I took a day off and set out for the bog with a sharp spade, a hay knife, a picnic bag, two children, and intructions on how to clear the sod over a bank of turf. It was a beautiful early June day. The bank, or layer of thick grass covering it, had to be cleared from the top before it would be possible to cut through the soft brown turf underneath.

I had heard many times of the romanticism of the bog, of clearing a bank in the sunshine, of cutting and stacking the turf, of picnics, how nothing tasted quite the same or nothing was quite so enjoyable. It may be all that in hindsight but to actually do it was sheer murder.

I started by putting the tip of the sharp spade onto the first piece of grass I would have to cut out. When I stamped down with my right foot I nearly broke another ankle. Romance of the bog was forgotten as I got on my knees and drove the hay knife, a huge, sharp, saw-like instrument, through the matted dry grass. Four steps back from the edge of the bank I turned the knife and cut a line parallel for about sixty feet and then back in towards the bank. It was then I had to try to get the spade through the matted, concrete-like surface and toss the sods, in the shape of blocks, into the space left in front from the last cutting, years before.

For the whole day I worked on it, helped by the two children, one forever hysterically dodging vampire flies, the other always standing in the wrong place in the middle of a wilderness.

Around lunchtime we stopped for tea and we fried sausages on a pan over dry pieces of turf on the tar road beside the bog. Maybe I was wrong about one thing in connection with the bog, sausages never tasted better. In the evening when I turned to look along the bank I could see that it would take another day to clear enough for Marty to cut the following Saturday. Every part of me ached and my hands were covered with blisters like balloons. We put the implements into the car as dusk fell and headed home, to be met at the door by Bernie who gasped at the dirt of the three urchins who stood on her mat. After baths and something to eat, we struggled wearily into bed.

The next evening, after my day's work, I went back on my own and gingerly started to clear the rest of the bank until the blisters on my hands burst and I could forget them. It was a little easier but still hard exhausting work. I also heard the cuckoo for the first time in my life, even if I was the last person in Clare to do so.

The following Saturday I collected Marty at seven in the morning and we drove in sleepy silence to the bog. Thankfully it was an overcast day. On the bog a light mist lay over the small hillocks and cut-out banks, with no sound save for the birds in the few trees along the bog road.

I was conscious that, with Marty coming to look at the bank I had cleared, in his eyes the honour of Dublin was at stake. If there was anything wrong with the surface, if it proved in any way more difficult to cut than in his forty previous years of doing so, it would be put down to the ineptitude of a city person on the bog.

Marty sprang from the car like a young pup and headed for the bank. When I reached him with the slean and forks he was pacing the top, stroking his chin in thought. "Well, is it cleared enough?" I asked. He shook his head, "Very wide, very wide". I shrugged. "Oh it's fine, it's fine", he said. Fine. I had passed the test, with compliments to boot. Now all I had to do was keep up with him. As he cut, I picked up the heavy, mud-like sods with a fork and put them out to dry. I was determined not to flag. After spending so much time on the bog on my own preparing for the maestro I was not about to fall at the last hurdle.

The man was an animal. It's no wonder he's in such demand to help on the bog. He never stopped, except to eat the food I had brought, which is a normal part of the fee. After eating it in silence, he was up like a ginnet and cutting sods again, which had me scurrying to catch up, having delayed to do the normal things with food, like chewing. But I did keep up, although I paid for my pride over the following days. We finished about half six that evening. Ten hours of solid physical work. It nearly killed me but he was as fresh leaving as when we had arrived.

I managed to hold onto the wheel as I drove home. Having washed up, and received my quota of pity, I went west to Jim to tell him that we had cut the turf. I still wasn't sure whether I should thank or murder him for its use. Marty lives in the most white-washed cottage you're likely to see, between ourselves and Connolly's. As I trudged past his house, looking as if I had just returned from a day with a chain gang, I heard a shout from his haggard where he stood leaning on a spade in the evening gloom. " Are you stiff boy?" he laughed. He was digging another ridge to plant carrots.

Chapter 18

G radually the number of people who wanted to move to west Clare from Dublin began to mount. It was becoming obvious that what up to now had been a one man movement could no longer be run by one person on their own. By the end of summer 1991 over 900 families had expressed an interest in moving to the West. Sixty-five famlies had already moved and the scale of the whole thing could no longer be sustained by Jim Connolly on a voluntary basis, while he also worked for himself as a sculptor.

It was against this background that the idea for a voluntary agency was first thought up by Jim. The dream became a reality on the 22nd of August 1991 when Rural Resettlement Irl Ltd was launched during the Merriman school in Lisdoonvarna. It was almost exactly a year to the day since we had moved to Kilbaha. I was asked by Jim to become one of the directors and was very happy to do so.

The main thing now was to get decent homes for those who wished to move and to obtain some government funding Those who had moved had handed back over one million pounds in local authority housing without a penny of central funding being given to help them rehouse. Later on the Government would recognise the value of the work and fund administration of the organisation.

At the start, Rural Resettlement was given a private donation from a Dublin businessman which enabled it to buy a small car and employ Sr Carmel Kehoe as a field officer to visit the families and to promote the organisation nationwide. Caroline Haugh, a girl from Kilkee, was employed as a secretary and computer operator for the machine which was also a donation. Sr Carmel was another resident for Kilbaha as she rented a house in the village.

I have to confess that I was a little wary of Carmel before I got to know her. My experience of nuns was very limited. For a short time as a young teenager I sold newspapers for a local newsagents near where I lived. One of our ports of call was the old folks home run by the Little Sisters of The Poor and it was one of the places to get in and out of quickly. My memories of it are of brief glimpses of old people, hovered over by black and white garmented figures. Later, two of these Sisters of The Poor used to call collecting for the order in a shop we had in Kilmainham. I don't know whether it was a stipulation of their order that they should be little Sisters, but I never saw any of them that were over five feet, except the Reverend Mother. They also seemed to have a doll-like appearance and a way of not quite being present, except in body, as they took the donations. It was as if they had something better to do or some place better to be, heaven I suppose. The point of the above is that Carmel was a very un-nun like nun and a great asset for R.R.I..

Aside from the families moving, most people who visit the county of Clare only ever go to the well known places such as Doolin, the Cliffs of Moher or Lisdoonvarna. We have yet to visit any of them save for a short evening stay in Lisdoonvarna for the launch of Rural Resettlement. The Loop and the surrounding area were enough to be going on with, and being lucky enough to get work after being in the area for only a short time, we didn't have much time to go exploring.

There was, however, one case of exploration close to home. It came about because of my involvement with the history research and my ever hopeful attitude of some day becoming rich, by the easiest and legitimate means possible.

Having discovered that four castles originally stood on the peninsula, we had to start trying to establish such things as the date of construction and the resident families. One of these castles, no longer standing, was a tower house on the north side of the peninsula near Kilkee, known as Dunlicky Castle. As we researched more and more into its history we came up with references to it being the stronghold of a pirate, one of the McMahon family. The local legend was that he would raid ships along the west coast and retreat to the sanctuary of Dunlicky. He did this by supposedly sailing his ship into the mouth of a cave to the east of the castle. This cave was rumoured to run underground from the base of the cliff to a safe place within the walls. The first relating of the story was from about the beginning of the 17th century and each century thereafter threw up these rumours of treasure being buried in the vicinity of the cave or castle.

In the last century, in fact, the newspapers reported the digging of the area of the castle site for treasure over a three-day period by about fifty men using spades. This search came to an abrupt end when there was a dispute among the diggers about the area to be dug and groups of them set about sinking their spades into each other instead.

I was indiscreet enough to speak of wishing to see the entrance to the cave and maybe explore its interior. Even when our archaeologist, Robert, informed me that these rumours existed of many Irish castles, my mental image of a wooden treasure chest half buried in sand with jewellery and Spanish gold coins spilling out still persisted. He warned me against further pursuance on the grounds of illegality and washed his hands of my treasure talk.

One evening in Jenny's I talked of my idea of having a look at the cave to the Pirate. The Pirate, as already mentioned, is a lobster fisherman and his knowledge of the coastline would prove invaluable if I should ever wish to stop daydreaming and go and look for myself. " Paul, I'll have a look along there the next time I'm in the area and I'll see if we can get in."

A few weeks later, having forgotten I mentioned the treasure, I was surprised when the Pirate, and another visitor and part-time fisherman named James, sat beside me on a Sunday evening in Jenny's to talk of the Castle. " We have something to show you", the Pirate whispered and furtively slipped a small package along the table, telling me to open it. " What is it? " " Ssh," James said, " we were up at your castle this morning," and he nodded for me to open the parcel. When spread on the table I saw a small brass coin and what looked like an old compass. " Proves it, without doubt. There's something up there alright ," James said. Having looked closely at the coin and compass I thought it unlikely that a pirate stronghold of the sixteenth century would have a Victorian penny and a compass with the year 1916 stamped on it, but I kept my suspicions to myself. It seemed more unlikely that these two would imagine it was proof of a pirate treasure. I asked few questions but put on a suitably impressed demeanor. When I could get a chance to get away from them, I asked Jenny if the Pirate had been out fishing that day. " No he hasn't been out at all, too rough." It confirmed what I suspected from the day's weather.

The Pirate had been well aware of the date on the items, he owned them. He was also well aware of the dates of the habitation of the castle. When I put this to him he soon admitted that he had been in Jenny's all day and no-where near the castle. James, he said, had been the prime mover in getting me to swallow the story of the false treasure. He asked me to keep up the pretence however, so for weeks after, when meeting both of them in company, I would plead with the Pirate to take me out to check the cave, saying I now had the use of a metal detector and would almost certainly find more. The Pirate acted his part of indifference with aplomb and James was a master at dismissing my amateur treasure hunting plans.

Chapter 19

One thing which soon becomes apparent to visitors and non-visitors alike is that no social function whatsoever starts on time in West Clare. It is always advisable to take the attitude locals do on being told the venue and time of some social event. Many times I've heard remarks and conversations as follows with regard to an evening out. " What time does it start at?" " Eight o'clock it says." " It'll be nine so." " Half I'd say." And both parties would agree to arrive an hour and a half after the advertised starting time, just as it begins in fact.

Many times over our early years we have made the mistake of being at social functions on time only to sit in solitude while the band set up, the ladies with sandwiches arrived or the proprietors set out the chairs. And naturally as the night begins later, it therefore has to end later. Turning a blind eye to the norms of the city, the country area just gets on with its own way of life.

In summer farmers and their helpers, who have worked for fourteen hours in the sun, are not about to worry about having a few well deserved drinks after the hours that the city lives with, but the country can't afford to. Locals don't expect the country publican to worry about it either. For myself the whole beauty of having a drink after hours was the illicit nature of it. With the farming community, having a pint after hours is the only time they can spare. That of course is not to say that in every bar in West Clare on every night of the year you can get a drink after eleven thirty or that every farmer is in them. There are some pubs where on an occasional night you don't have to rush, but you will have to find them for yourself.

Incidents which brought home the difference from city hours as opposed to country hours occurred in towns near to us when we were having occasional nights out. On one such evening on entering one of the music pubs in Kilkee we were asked for a pound cover charge. Now a pound cover charge into this particular pub was very little for the music provided, but being a stranger with city habits I pointed out that it was now almost eleven thirty. "You're right there", the doorman said looking at his watch. " But what time do you close?" I asked. " About October", he answered.

In another town a bar owner told me that he had owned the place for five years and had yet to call time on any night. I must finish this subject by pointing out that all the above is hearsay and could not, I hope, be substantiated in a court of law, as it was heard by a person or persons under the influence.

While on the subject of towns, Kilkee and Kilrush are the nearest ones to where we live on the Loop Head peninsula. Kilkee is about thirteen miles west, with Kilrush a further eight. Other than for the drive into them, maybe once a week, between them we can get the items that the two local shops don't have, such as some varieties of meat, items from the chemist, or even a hair cut. Therefore the butcher, the chemist and the barber are mainly what draw us to these places of habitation as well as the novelty of a trip to town.

All of these local businessmen are characters in their own right. The chemist and the butcher we normally frequent are situated in Kilkee while my barber has his premises in Kilrush. The pharmacy in Kilkee is owned by John and Elizabeth Williams, but is generally known as Williams. They also run a hardware and builders providers. Williams are a successful but easy going business, as we often found when ordering fuel or other items and not being in a position to immediately pay. There was never a problem. John Williams is also, I discovered, the first to be tapped, as we called it in Dublin, when some fund raising event is in the offing.

One of the butchers we stumbled on after a short time in the area was Michael Nolan, an immediately likeable rogue who has his shop on the main street in Kilkee. When shopping for meat with him it's advisable to have little idea of what you are seeking and plenty of time to do it. We have often gone in with the sole intention of buying a pound of sausages and come out with a turkey or lumps of meat which we could hardly carry. In his shop nothing seems to have a price and everything from rashers to cuts of beef is charged at a pound per lb. All the above when wrapped is put on the scales together and worked out in Michael's cash register mind. Invariably when weighed he will look you in the eye and with mock seriousness inquire, " Have you two fivers on you?" When they are handed over another handful of sausages, a lump of black pudding or a few rashers are thrown into the bag before it is hefted over the counter. "Can ye manage that now folks?"

My tonsorial artist has his premises on the square in Kilrush and whatever about the layout of the interior he is the best barber who has ever cut my hair. John the Barber, while being the best, is also one of the quickest, and you are hardly rested before he is brushing your neck and dusting you off. What makes his such an unusual premises is his passion for bird-watching and adoption of injured birds of prey. All around his shop are the paraphernalia of his pastime.

Every available place in the shop is taken up by magazines, photos, tripods, binoculars and whatever else is needed for his outings. He struts about the debris in bare feet as he has an aversion to wearing shoes, qualifying it with the remark that, " These ones won't wear out so easily." Our two children love coming with me to see John the Bird-watcher, as they know him, from his visits to the local schools with his falcons and other lodgers. On visits, and after questioning on his premises about thc birds on his last visit to the school, our two children are given a lollipop from his stock for erratic children.

While settling in and getting to know all of the people we met in the West Clare area there were of course many disapointments. Of all the disappointments concerning our move, the greatest so far must have been the inability of our dog Todd to take to the rural way of life. The city must have been deep within him, because any time we let him loose he carried on in a way which would inevitably end up getting him run back to the big smoke.

We tried bringing him for walks on a lead down to the pier and were dragged over ditches and under gates by his amazing strength, as he tried to sort out the cows that came to look at him at the side of the field. On reaching the beach the very first time, we let him off his lead only for him to bound into the water and stay about three or four feet away from us in the tide. He then proceeded to skirt Kilbaha bay for miles while we coaxed, pleaded, cursed, and even tried to lassoe him with a rope, to get him back in.

On another occasion we foolishly allowed him off his rope outside the house to see if he might run about, get used to the place and then settle down to some sort of normal life. The first time we did he tore down our drive and turning east he scurried into our neighbours milking parlour just as the cows were being connected up to the milking machines. He then set about causing pandemonium and bringing production to a standstill by running in and out between the cows feet. We got him out with his life but realised that serious measures would have to be taken if we were to have any peace at all.

Consulting some local dog owners and animal experts resulted in very odd suggestions. These varied from the drastic one of castration to the unbelievable one of tossing him from the cliffs at the Bridges at Ross. The first we discounted and the second we ignored. We rang the I.S.P.C.A. in Ennis for advice and were told that as he was a small dog he would very likely be placed with a family in the town if we wanted to leave him in. The next phase was to get the children to agree, which to our surprise proved quite easy. When explained to Susan one evening she realised it would be better for him and agreed to his move. On telling Stephen of the imminent departure of his dog he screwed up his face and said, " O.K., but can we get a cat."

Todd was placed in a seat of prominence beside me in the car, and for the first time in his life didn't budge for the whole journey. If only he had behaved anything like it during the previous year we would not be making this journey in the first place. He must have guessed somewhere in his doggie brain that something unusual was afoot, probably because we weren't shouting at him. I suppose he really wasn't a bad dog, just mad.

When I reached the animal shelter in Ennis the warden was out so I took Todd for a short walk around the rough ground surrounding the shelter. He stuck to my heels on his lead like a champion from Crufts, again for the first time ever. I was almost about to pick him up and put him back in the car when the warden arrived. " So this is the little fella?" he said calling Todd who trotted over to him. There was no fear of his behaving even a little badly to show the warden the reason for his visit. I asked the warden to phone us if a family didn't take him as we would not want him to be put down. He promised to do so and picked him up as I got back into the car. Pulling away I saw Todd trying to lick his face and for once, after all the bother of owning him, I was sorry to see him go. I remembered cycling with him as a pup in the inside of my jacket two years before, to the Blue Cross ambulance, which parked in Ballyfermot, to have him vaccinated. The first casualty of our move.

We never did get a phone call from the I.S.P.C.A. so we presume he must have got a bed for himself somewhere in the town to which he would have been better suited. Soon after, Lassie, the next door neighbours sheepdog had four pups in our hay barn and at least these did not chase cattle. Todd is probably laid up somewhere comfortably in Ennis with a loving family.

Chapter 20

When the first cold winds of the second winter in Kilbaha began to blow in across the peninsula, there was a definite feeling of sadness that the summer was again gone and we were looking towards the long nights and dark months ahead. The previous winter had been a type of initiation test which we had determined to pass without complaint. The many questions of whether we would weather the West Clare storms had been answered. This time we were facing the winter as locals and viewed its approach as they did.

We had prepared for it as we had never thought of doing when living in the city. We had stocked up on fuel and taken to the beaches more often to collect wood, and anything else that would burn. Even earlier than the wind, the coming of the cold had been heralded, when on blackberry picking trips in the fields behind the house, the scent of burning turf from the cottages below drifted over the high ground. On September evenings we could not go out without wrapping in coats and jumpers. But to us the real sign was when the kids again asked for the hot water bottles to be put in their beds.

Our neighbour Marty's forecasts became gleefully gloomier and gloomier and with the constant winds and rain of our second winter we recognised how mild the last one had been, even if it did have one of the most severest February storms ever. But if you have a good turf fire going and can keep the house warm it can be comfortable no matter where you are. We were, and we had the scenic views. I can never cease to talk of the beauty of the West Clare coastline on the Loop. In summer easy to love and in winter, wild, multi-coloured sea, foaming along grey green land and rock. The peace, in winter, other than the noise of the wind, is overpowering. No longer the tractor races of the silage cutting summer, or the convoys during the later hay cutting, or even the usual cows bellowing each morning. All that had been the preparation by the farming community for the quiet winter feeding of the animals. The slatted houses where the cattle would spend the cold months were steamingly full.

During that winter many mornings and evenings, when storms blew in, the electricity would be cut off, with the lines blown down from the wooden poles. It was a miracle to me when looking out at the storms how the E.S.B. workers could ever get the lines back up on the poles which were blown almost horizontal to the ditches by the wind. Occasionally the water supply to the house would also be cut off and we would have to resort to using water from the old well at the top of the driveway. After boiling and having removed the twigs, leaves and the odd dead insect from the water it tasted fine.

Also during the many storms, buckets of vegetables and potatoes would be left up by Marty or Paddy Ban. Any visits in the winter were welcome and the noise of a car on the driveway was a hoped for sound to break the monotony. And, naturally, west of Ireland weather always tried to confuse us. Going to bed in winter on a November evening we might wake to glorious spring-like weather the next morning.

All the vegetables of our second year were now harvested and the ridges of spuds were now a large heap in a box in the corner of the cabin above our house. I should really have put them in bags, but, trying to be over rural, I had again placed them in a pit which later became a damp hole where they lasted for most of the winter. However, as well as feeding us I noticed, when coming towards the end of the harvest, that they were also feeding a multitude of smaller creatures, if the nips and bites were anything to go by. Also, hung about the cabin from the wooden rafters were strings of sweet smelling onions. These also lasted most of the winter but towards the end became soft and had to be dumped. The peas, beans, sprouts etc were frozen and lasted us through the dark months.

In late autumn, while all the normality of living in the country was going on, the resettlement scheme which had brought us in the first place was making news in places further afield. One evening Jim Connolly phoned us to say that a German T.V. crew were coming to the area to film and interview some of the resettled families. He immediately gauged my uninterested reaction for he continued, "They're also going to pay." Mercenary to the last, I volunteered to help in any way I could.

They interviewed myself and Bernie, standing on our doorstep, then myself standing in the aftermath of the autumn harvest in the haggard below the house. Having gone through the list of veg I had grown I had pointed to the cabin where the abundant harvest was now stored.

" Could we film there you think please?" the lady interviewer asked. Certainly I assured them, only too glad to show off my crop. When we reached the cabin I led them into my vegetable store, proudly pointing out the varieties, the small pile of spuds in the corner and the strings of onions hanging from the roof. The lady interviewer looked around and began to laugh. " What is it?" I asked. " Oh nothing", she said, "it is just the way you talk I think the shed would be full of vegetables." "It is to me", I said, my gardener's ego dented. Eventually they had me emerge from the shed for take after take with a string of onions held aloft and a stupid grin on my face. I wasn't surprised when they didn't use any of it in the final programme. We were paid anyway and thankfully the image of my half-witted grin while holding up the onions wasn't seen across Germany.

Very soon after the Germans, the B.B.C. decided to make a half-hour programme on the resettlement scheme for their Country File series. They arranged all the details with Jim and informed him that they would, as always, be taking their time to get it right. They certainly did that. They were professional and repetitive to their finger tips. The programme showed why, and just how good they were.

The B.B.C. crew arrived on a Friday evening in early winter and were lucky enough to land there on one of the busiest social evenings in Haiers bar. It was a benefit night for a charity organisation and an appearance by the Bannermen, a Clare group who specialised in set dancing music. The B.B.C. crew were delighted and invited the Dublin families in the area to attend. For hours they filmed us in every conceivable stance. The dancing was filmed from every angle, including the camera man lying on the floor. The McMahons, the Fagins, the O'Briens and ourselves were all caught in compromising positions, except in my own case, that of staged set dancing. An old leg injury can be a great asset at times.

The crew, with a camera and sound man from Dublin, stayed in the area for three days. The presenter Rupert and the producer Jo Skarsby were both English. On the day after the dance they came to interview us, setting up huge powerful lights outside every window of the house. They interviewed ourselves and the children with great professionalism. The next day they filmed us walking along the cliff top at Ross with the children. The wind obligingly came out on cue also. They left the following day and the programme was awaited with keen interest. It was shown a few Sundays later. It was an excellent piece of work and the best we had seen on the scheme so far. A half hour programme after three days of solid filming. The professionalism showed with every frame.

The second year in Clare

The velocity with which time flies is infinite , as is most apparent to those who look back.

Seneca

Chapter 21

As the history project was finishing during the winter of 1991 and spring of 1992 I had begun to write the first of the fourteen chapters of the book on it. The book would eventually be called '*Cuchulain's Leap*'. The name Loop Head is really a misnomer of the ancient Irish name 'Cean Leime' or Leap Head. The story of its origin is far too long to be gone into here but suffice to say that it was a suitable name for the book. My idea had been to sit down and write the book as we were finishing the research between January and March. Luckily I had been told by people in FAS, who were overseeing the project and who knew about these things, to get working on it before Christmas.

The research had taken myself and the young trainees to many new places for all of us. We practically lived in the local library in Kilkee. Many more times we had to make the fifty-mile journey to the excellent reference library in Ennis. As well as this we had pored over the two hundred years of newspapers in the *Clare Champion* offices in Ennis. Dublin was also visited on many occasions by all the trainees and myself. While there we researched material on the peninsula in the National Archive at the Four Courts, the National Library, the Royal Hospital, Kilmainham Goal, Trinity College and many others. While I may have been hampered by the fact that research like this was new to me, it was nothing compared to some of the young Clare trainees, who had never even been to Dublin. But between us we managed to get along.

When we had done all we possibly could in the research line, when we had interviewed all the people possible, when all the photos had been taken by our volunteer photographer Paddy Flanagan, it was time to sit down and write the history of the parishes of Carrigaholt and Cross.

From September to March of the following year, on most nights of the week, I would come home from the history course each evening and, after dinner and the six o'clock news, I would sit until eleven thirty or so writing the book. The saving grace was that Bernie had finished work the previous August and, while she looked after the children, their homework and the house, I could turn my full attention to writing. Many nights, when the coming of winter and bad weather kept the children indoors, they would play noisily about the room, where I sat in total oblivion to the noise around me. I was too engrossed to even stop when they occasionally spread a sheet over the table where I worked and played tents underneath. Just once they didn't move the layers of pages spread in organised chaos in front of me.

There was so much to check and sort and recheck that a bomb would not have moved me. With the book to write, trying to fill the days of seven female trainees, helping with the running of Rural Resettlement and all the media interest that involved, as well as writing another comedy script for the youth club, I had never been so busy at any time in my life. To think that it had started with a dream of a quiet life in the country. I had envied people enjoying their work and being busy, and now for once I had so much to do that I couldn't even take an hour off.

By Christmas I had half of the book written and Robert, our archaeologist, was almost finished his surveying and would write the first chapter on topography and archaeology in the early new year. It was time for a rest.

The children no longer enquired if Santa would make it to the West coast. Kilbaha was now the centre of the world as far as they were concerned and they knew he would not dare to go anywhere else first. They had even planned his route which would roughly work out North Pole, Kilbaha and then on to the rest of the kids on earth.

The second Christmas we again missed the looked-forward-to Wren, not because of the weather this year, but because of us driving to Dublin on Christmas day as my sister Marie, her husband Mick, and their family were home on holiday from Australia and our extended family were getting together for a knees up. We didn't want to leave before Christmas morning in case Santa would get mixed up with where we lived.

On returning from Dublin it was back to work straight away to finish the book, broken only by a visit from the Aussies who had come to unwind from the rigours of the winter social scene in Dublin. I'm afraid they had been misinformed about the Clare social scene and they returned to Dublin for a well earned rest.

By March the history book was finished and we were happy enough with the end result. We had given many people chapters to read on subjects they were familiar with and had fixed up the small problems before letting it go to the printers. It was an end to another part of our new life in West Clare when we handed over the manuscript and photographs to the *Clare Champion* on a Friday evening, thus ending the course officially. The following week FAS came to collect all the equipment and the portacabin at Bella was empty and lonely when I looked around the rooms on the last day before closing it for good. I thought back to the first eventful day there, to all the noisy good humoured work, the cold tired days, the frustration and the discoveries. Everything that had happened over a year in the building came flooding back before I pulled the door shut and closed the lock. To this day the premises at Bella stand empty and are beginning to revert to their former neglected state. Each time I pass there is a certain amount of sadness at the waste of it and the memories of what we achieved there.

Chapter 22

By mid June, after reading the proofs, dotting the i's and crossing the t's, the history of Carrigaholt and Cross- *Cuchulain's Leap*- arrived in Kilbaha. It was a close run thing, however. The *Clare Champion* managed to get 100 of the 500 copies to us on the evening of the launch. I collected them outside Haicr's Bar in Kilbaha, to where they were delivered by the *Champion's* van. Opening the cardboard box which contained a years work was not a thing I would care to do all that often. We had orders for 200, a large crowd had been invited to the launch in Kilkee and as yet I hadn't seen the finished article. When I grasped the first copy in my hand I saw I needn't have worried. There must be no better feel or smell than that of a brand new hard-back book. And how exciting to see your own name on the dust cover I brought the books and the accompanying covers home. Before we got ready to go to the launch, we all sat, including my mother and father who had come for the occasion, and put the covers carefully on each book.

To officially launch the book we were lucky to get the one person we had really tried for, Jim Kemmy. As well as being a noted historian Jim was also the Mayor of Limerick. In the hotel that evening, when he stood to give his speech he talked knowledgeably on every chapter. No one would have believed that he had only received a copy of the book that morning.

After the speeches the large crowd surged forward and the hundred copies were gone within hour. The sweat was pouring off me as I tried to sign each copy thrust into my hand while the former trainees on the course collected the money. The 500 copies were sold within 6 weeks and the whole thing was a surprising success to everyone concerned.

Now the plan was to have a bit of a break and enjoy the Loop Head for some of the summer, while all the time looking out for some work. The month of May that year was one of the warmest recorded, June was one of the wettest and a foretaste of the rest of the year. I had had little time for the garden but was still able to put in six ridges of spuds, as well as peas, onions, carrots and swedes. The most successful were the spuds, even though blight got to them in the bad summer weather. Luckily enough they didn't rot in the ground, only stopped growing. We were still eating them the following April.

Also during the summer of 1992 the Clare football team, having won the Munster Championship, had to play the winners of Leinster. That year it was Dublin. In my household there was divided loyalty, with the count two for Clare, one for Dublin, and one without interest. The two children had long before adopted the colours of their native county, I was uninterested, unless for devilment, and Bernie was a rowdy Dublin supporter. She had wanted to fly a navy and blue flag from our hilltop to signify her support for the Dubs but the children would have none of it. Failing that I had to tie the Dublin colours to the car on the morning of the match as I drove them to mass. A braver more foolish gesture could not have been imagined. Throughout the county a fired up partisan attitude prevailed for the first Clare participation in an All-Ireland semi-final in seventy-five years. There were a few odd looks outside the church, some shouts, and many fists raised in laughter at the audacity.

Of course Dublin won the match. That evening I just had to spend some time in Jennie's, gloating, sympathetically though, as all modest winners should. A few weeks later, continuing my new found support for the Dublin team, they were whipped by the lads from Donegal in the All-Ireland Final. I had to return to the place of former glory and take it on the chin, as the crowd in Jennie's cheered every Donegal point on the highlight's of the match that night, all in my direction.

Otherwise summer passed with the usual rhythm of farming in a country area. Now, however, I had a better idea of what was going on. I could talk about silage and how it was cut. I had learned about calving time and the luck of twins, the wet hay and red water and slatted houses and slurry. Yes, we knew what slurry and its spreading was all about. The aroma drifted up to our high position when the wind was blowing in the right direction, and on the Loop the wind always blows, in every direction.

Chapter 23

It was early July and the week when all of Clare were celebrating
the winning of the first Munster Championship after a gap of
seventy-five years. The Kilbaha area was in a state of sadness
having buried a young man who was literally a friend to all who lived
there.

Martin Fennell, a farmer and part time fisherman, was lost at sea on the
evening of Friday, July 10th, 1992. The place where his small boat
went down is just under the cliffs at Fodry where he was born and his
parents still live.

That Friday had been an odd day with regard to the weather and the sea
about the Loop. It was beautiful and sunny for most of the day, yet
across the land from us on the coast at Ross and Fodry the sea was
white-capped and rough, with a larger swell than was usual for sunny
weather. For the first time since we had moved, on taking the children
to swim behind the pier, Kathleen Connolly had decided that the swell
was too dangerous and brought them home.

That evening, with the sun still shining brightly, Bernie and I decided
not to take our usual walk to the pier but to turn west and walk the
three miles or so toward the lighthouse. We passed Connolly's where
the kids were playing with their friends.

It was about seven thirty and after about a mile we noticed a rescue
helicopter from Shannon hovering over the cliffs at Ross and Fodry. A
helicopter in the area is not an unusual sight as Shannon rescue, and,
occasionally, Irish Lights helicopters are seen over the peninsula. It
was only on the way back when meeting Mrs Murray, a local farmer's
wife, that we were told that Martin's small out-board lobster boat had

been reported capsised and the family had rang for the marine rescue whose helicopter was now hovering. On the way back down the Loop road we saw the helicopter rise into the air and head back east towards Shannon. Everyone assumed that the alert was over, but when the copter returned a short time later the spirits of those watching from our side of the peninsula sank.

As the night wore on the full story of what had happened began to be pieced together from various people who had been helping in the search. Martin had gone fishing for lobster that day and his father, who lived on the shore overlooking his strings of pots at Fodry, had seen him in at the cliff face in the early afternoon. Later on, about six thirty, his small boat was seen capsised in the rough swells near the cliff face. At first nobody was too concerned about Martin as he had often been in scrapes at sea and had got home safely. He was an excellent swimmer, had many hours scuba diving, and was as strong as a horse to boot.

Only the previous Sunday his out-board engine had cut out while at sea and he had to attempt to row almost ten miles to get back to where he usually anchored. When he found that it might take him all night he had decided to send up a flare. The Kilkee Marine rescue had come out and towed him into safety. The following day I had to pass Martin's house, and, as he sat outside stripping his boat engine, he laughed and held up a small strip of cracked rubber to me. " That's the only feckin thing that stopped me yesterday, isn't it the divil".

After the Kilkee rescue had towed him in that evening, some of the lads, all voluntary, were made to accompany Martin to Jenny's where a good night was had by all, with him getting his saviours a few well-earned pints. The next day, as he sat fixing the engine, he was still guzzling minerals in memory of it. When I heard that they were looking for him on that Friday evening I presumed it was the same small piece of rubber that had put him out of action.

As complete darkness fell that Friday evening, the lads from Shannon and Kilkee rescue had to call off the search. Those on shore kept the vigil, hoping that he sat huddled on some rocky ledge waiting to be hauled up. Before finally going to bed that night I looked across at the car lights and flash lamps along the beach and on the cliff tops and felt useless.

The following morning, when he hadn't been found, only the family held out any real hope, yet the divers from Kilkee, and many other places, as well as the Marine rescue, continued to search relentlessly. For four days over one hundred divers spent hours in the dark and dangerous waters on the north side of the Loop searching for Martin's body. Most of them left jobs and farms to spend hour after hour in the cold water so the family could bury Martin and be at peace. The fishermen of the area stopped all work and plied up and down the coast in search of their friend.

Clues to what happened began to emerge. His oilskins, which he usually wore, were found floating in the water. It seemed that he had been able to remove them, along with other clothing later found, and attempt to swim ashore. It was still hoped that he might be lying injured somewhere along the shore. The RTE and Clare FM radio news noted the search for a lone fisherman off the Loop head peninsula and you felt yourself wanting to say to the dispassionate voice that it wasn't a lone fisherman, it was Martin Fennell, the ever smiling west Clare man who was our friend. If he had strolled up from the sea the following Monday with his gear over his shoulder no one would have been surprised.

On Tuesday, the 14th of July, they found Martin's body. He had tried to swim to shore, some of the fishermen even surmising that he may have sat on the overturned boat before losing patience or getting hungry and striking out for home. When he was found, with a kind of disbelief, we accepted.

The funeral from Kilkee to the church at Moneen near Kilbaha was the biggest in living memory. Outside the church that windy Thursday morning I saw the largest crowd gathered in one place since we had moved to Clare.

The blowing of the wind drowned out the sound of the mass from within to all who could not gain entry to the church, yet they stood in complete silence. Many people had to leave the church, heads bowed in sorrow, because of the emotion and the huge numbers packed inside. Just before the coffin was expected to be brought out a line of about thirty to forty local fishermen stood to each side of the gateway, large oars pointed straight to the grey sky in salute and still not a sound but the wind. For a long time, while every person in the church lined to extend their sympathy to the family, the fishermen stood quietly, holding their oars rigid in the breeze. The coffin was carried the half mile to the old cemetery at Kiltrellig which overlooks Kilbaha Bay. As the final prayers were said over the grave I saw men, women and even children move quietly from the grave-side to cry in silence.

After the funeral some of the large crowd went to Haiers or Jenny's. No one knew quite how to behave. Every so often a relative or friend would break down. It was unlike any of the usual funerals of older people in the area whose death was accepted because of their age. The wake went on quietly for the afternoon and, through tiredness and drink, the farmers and fishermen slowly drifted away. As they did one of the fishermen stood and began to sing in a low voice the first verse of 'Fiddlers Green', Martins song, which he had sang on many nights in Jenny's. Most of those there sang it loudly or listened as the last notes of the final verse died away. Then they all left. The morning of Martins funeral another friend, an elderly man, Joe Gibson, died. We had been introduced to Joe the first day we had come to see the house in Kilbaha and he always had time for a talk on his evening walks near our house. He died in Ennis Hospital and was buried in Kiltrellig cemetery, a little east of where Martin lay. On the way from another funeral in that little graveyard the same week, I passed where the younger man's newly dug grave was. Flowers of every shape and colour lay in a large mound over and around the freshly dug soil of Martin's grave. Already, after only two days, the blossoms had lost the freshness of the funeral day and I thought of Martin again, his red beaming face with thick glasses, with arm raised to bang down his winning card at '45' in Jenny's. Many people will miss him very much, as will we.

Chapter 24

In the month of August 1992 our life was set to change again without us knowing. The second anniversary of our move to the West had passed without any formality. The kids would be going back to school soon again to start their third term and we were still renting the house to which we had moved.

I had been picking up bits of work in the locality, driving buses for a local firm to all sorts of functions, including bingo in Ennistymon. I sat behind all the patrons and played it for the first time with the free book given to all bus drivers. I tend to keep that a secret from the lads back in Dublin. Driving, or bingo, was not what I had come to Clare for, but money was sort of essential to buy most things and I was offered the work so took it gladly. I would get back to writing in the winter I told myself, but after the research for the previous one it was hard to motivate myself to start another project.

Rural Resettlement were also donated a truck about that time and occasionally I would travel to Dublin to bring a family to the west, staying overnight in my mother's and being paid expenses for the trip. So I was doing my little bit of driving, no writing, and not worrying about getting back to it for the moment.

I was still a director of Rural Resettlement and as summer drew to a close the number wishing to move was rising daily. At long last the scheme was about to get official recognition in the form of grants for administration from the Department of Environment and the E.C. The directors discussed the full-time employment of Sr Carmel as Field Officer and Caroline, who had been keeping the office going, along with Jim, as secretary. There was also discussion about employing an administrator on a full-time basis when funding allowed.

One evening in September Jim Connolly phoned me and asked if I could call to his house. This was unusual as we probably saw each other two or three times every day and our children lived in Connolly's during the summer.

I strolled down to see what it was he might want, thinking it might be a lift with a statue or some such thing. Sitting me formally on one of his kitchen chairs he said, " As Chairman of Rural Resettlement I am going to recommend to the board that when funding becomes available you should be offered the position of administrator." Simple as that. I told him that I would be glad to accept but I would like to talk to Bernie about it first. It was an offer of running a national organisation. I don't suppose many such positions were successfully secured in such a manner. But it wasn't such a dumb move after all. We were the second family to move, I had been on the board since its inception and over that time many of the families had become known to me, as well as our family becoming adept at dealing with the media. The rest I could learn from Jim. Bernie was unsure whether it was the right thing to do. She felt, and rightly, that dealing with families was never going to be an easy thing.

Eventually we agreed I should accept the offer and I told Jim, who said he would put it to the next meeting of the board. In my self-imposed absence from the meeting the board agreed with Jim and I was now employed again. Of course there was no money in it. I learned the job for three months on a voluntary basis while waiting for funding to come through and I was also available for work elsewhere should it arise. When I say I learned the job I may be speaking a little hastily. When you work with Jim Connolly and Rural Resettlement there are no two days the same. There is always a plan or a dream or a way of forwarding the organisation. When Jim goes for a long walk around the Loop I know that on his return we are going to be doing something new, maybe exciting, but definitely involving more work.

When I took over from Jim, doing the work on a daily basis which he had being doing after working a full day at his own job, I was amazed that he had had the time to fit it all in. Every day I would drop the children into school and then go to Connolly's where the Rural Resettlement office was located in their back porch. I would get home for lunch for about an hour, collect the kids at three, then go back and finish about five thirty.

Every day was busy. There were families wishing to move, houses to check, and the many other aspects of a new national organisation in the making. When I was offered the job the figure stood at seventy -

eight families moved to ten Irish counties with eleven hundred families on the waiting list. By the end of 1992 the figure had risen to eighty - five families moved to twelve counties with over fourteen hundred on the waiting list.

Although the figure of families moved had not greatly increased the number wishing to move had. This was because of the constant media interest in the scheme and the shortage of decent houses available for long-term lease. At the end of the year the scheme had featured on twelve T.V. programmes in Ireland and world-wide. Every day the post brought in new inquiries from all parts of Ireland, from Britain, America and even Australia and New Zealand. I'm still learning.

Chapter 25

S till learning. That could be said to describe our lives now in Clare. We are still learning. Learning to make friends, to know where people come from in the area. We are still learning to speak and understand the local dialect, the normal sayings, the way people in the area use the language. Our children had long been accustomed to all of that but it would take their parents a little longer.

Having walked most of the roads on the Loop when researching the history course there wasn't a road or a townland in the area that I didn't know. But when you haven't lived in an area all your life, what you learn in an academic exercise is not likely to stay as clear in your mind as if you are raised with it.

We have made friends. Long-lasting, good friends who will remain such wherever we are. People constantly ask how the locals took to us. Were we accepted? Was there ever any bad feelings? We didn't experience any adverse reaction and feel we are accepted. But we didn't suddenly wake up one morning and say to ourselves, 'now we feel accepted.' It was a gradual thing, the blending into the community on the West Clare peninsula.

Small things when looked at in isolation showed how we were becoming locals. Things such as not causing more than casual interest from locals when out walking. Being served in place in a que in the two local shops and not being made a fuss of. The hard-bitten card players taking no notice of my entry into Jennies of a Sunday evening. Or being told of the death or marriage of a local without them adding the address of the person mentioned.

We found that in the language we were accepted. When a neighbour tells us he is going 'east' and not adding 'to Kilkee.' Or they are going 'west' and not adding 'towards the lighthouse.' Or when some local moans to you of bad hay, or even the nuisance of tourists. And eventually, being introduced to someone by a local and them not adding after your name 'from Dublin.'

Being accepted varies according to who you meet. To many people we will always be the people from Dublin no matter how many generations our family may stay. And it is not a derogatory thing. Not in an area where a road is still called Kildare Road a hundred years after a native of that county lived and died in a house there. The house is long gone but people still know who bought the man's plough after his passing.

Had we changed? Were we still just the city people who had moved to the west of Ireland? We had not changed yet we had changed utterly. We were still the same family but we had grown by our experience. All that had happened to us in that short time would shape the way we lived and thought for the rest of our lives.

Nature would never again be something we were unaware of. It would never again be just an item to watch on T.V. or read about in the library. We were part of it, and the cycle of nature on the Loop Head peninsula was a part of us. Our lives would be ruled by it and not city hours and neon lights. And nature is real life after all.

We could never again live in a house where another family would disturb our life by the normal noise of living. To us now they would be living almost indecently close if behind the next wall. Space was important where it had not even been thought of before. Space and safety. The safety of not worrying about the dark. Of not thinking that every stranger was a threat to your family. The safety of using locks only to keep out pets, or the wind, or dust, or just for closing the door.

Everything hadn't been rosy. There had been trying times, times when we were short of money, times of feeling isolated and far away, times when we worried about having a house next year, or the year after. The greatest sorrow was not being in Dublin when Bernie's father was dying.

But all that we had originally listed back at the beginning of the dream of moving to the country as possible drawbacks we had overcome. We had experienced all that we expected we would, and soon we would have a new house of our own in Clare.

We had experienced change and we were happy with what we had done. Clare, a county we had never been in before our move, was an important place to us and always would be. The Loop Head was our home. We had grown to like and then love it. And in an odd way, from our small hill overlooking the Shannon to the south and the mighty Atlantic to the north yes, in a way, we had even grown to like the wind.